My First
Motivational Cursive
Handwriting Workbook

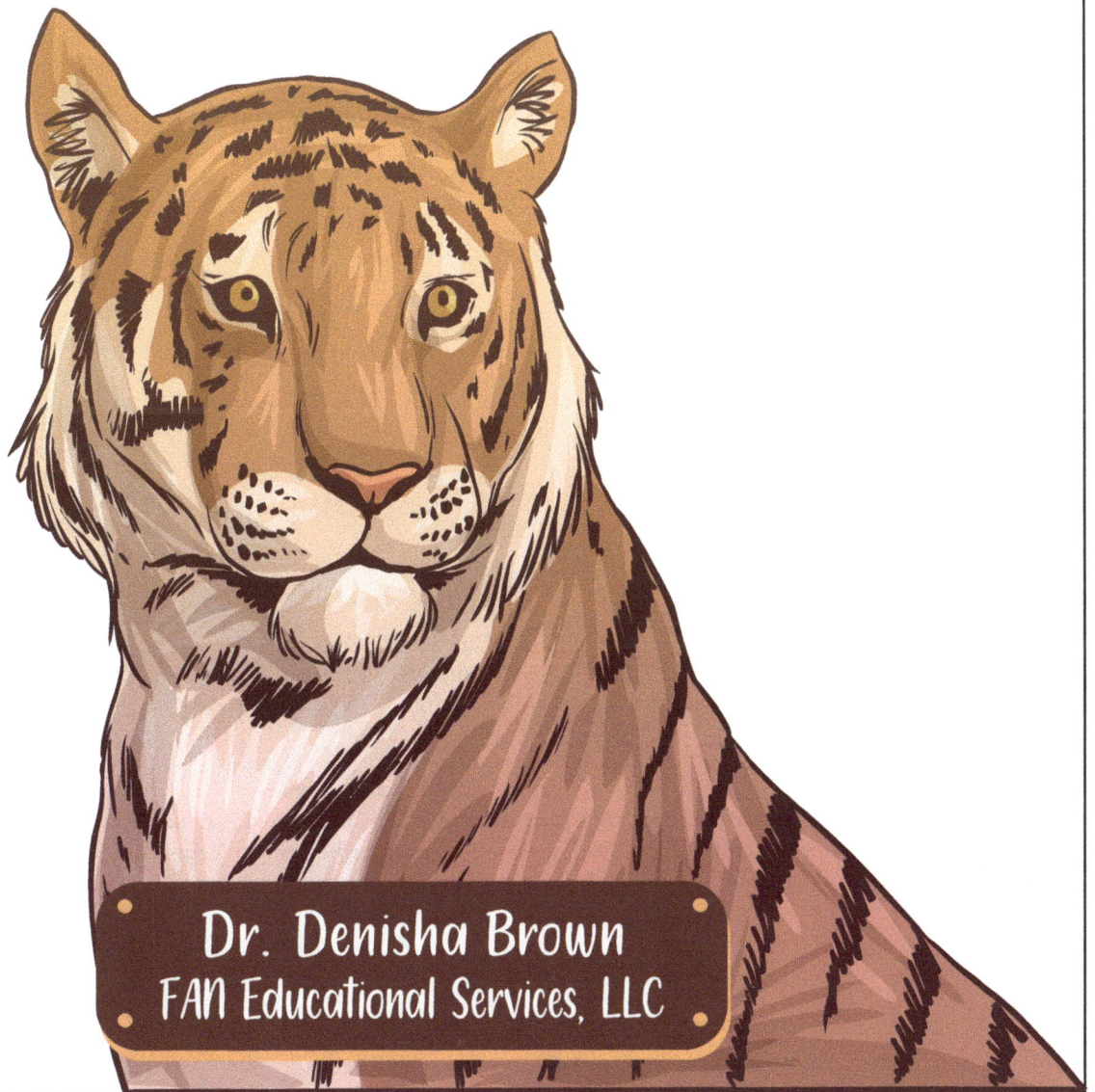

Dr. Denisha Brown
FAN Educational Services, LLC

MY FIRST MOTIVATIONAL
CURSIVE HANDWRITING WORKBOOK

This Book Belongs To:

_____

_____

Author's Message

Did you know that your child attains positive self-esteem by the age of 5? On the other hand, did you know that when your child becomes a teenager, their self-esteem reaches a state of little or no change? Therefore, speaking positively to your children and allowing children to speak positively is critical to shaping their self-esteem.

I am Dr. Denisha Brown, an educational leader and educational consultant. Throughout my career in Education, I have observed and researched the importance of building a child's self-esteem. Children often use the words "I can't" and lack the confidence to complete a given task. In addition to lacking confidence, many children have no knowledge of penmanship in cursive handwriting. This lack of knowing how to write in cursive could lead to the inability to obtain and sustain opportunities as children become adults. Therefore, I decided to combine motivational words and cursive handwriting practice in this workbook to build teenagers' self-esteem and increase their ability to write in cursive.

As we prepare to cultivate our children into future leaders for a global society, it is my vision that this motivational cursive handwriting workbook can assist in shaping their mindset. I hope this workbook provides cursive handwriting support for your teenager, teaches them new vocabulary, and builds their self-esteem and confidence to be the best scholar and citizen in today's society for years to come!

Let's spread positivity in the world!
Please share your work on social media using #Fan_Ed, #UniqueMe, #CoolTeensColor.

Dr. Brown

My First Cursive Handwriting Workbook was created to reinforce extra practice with cursive handwriting.

The purpose of the motivational words aligned with each alphabet is to increase the self-esteem of pre-teens and teenagers. It is vital that all children hear and receive 5 or more positive praises for every 1 corrective interaction for negative behavior. This workbook is going to help improve cursive handwriting skills, build vocabulary, and build your teen's self-esteem and confidence. I thank you for your purchase and hope you and your teen enjoys it.

Helpful Suggestions

1. Allow your teen to practice handwriting skills at least 20 minutes a day or 3 times a week.
2. If your teen struggles with making letters in cursive try practicing the basic shapes of cursive letters like loops and continous curves. This will allow your child to get familiar with the movement of cursive letter making.
3. Use the activity page to write 3 words that begin with the letter of practice. Then use each word in a sentence. Remember to write in cursive!
4. You can extend the activity page by challenging your teen to write 10 or more words and use each in a sentence writing in cursive.
5. Ask your teen to use the name of each animal on the correspondent coloring sheet in a sentence.
6. Have your teen say the Daily Affirmations to increase your teen's self-esteem and confidence.
7. Challenge your teen to create their own affirmations and post them in their room for encouragement and inspiration towards their goals and dreams.

Trace each letter or word. Practice writing each letter on your own.

A

A A A A A A

A A A A A A

A

A

Amazing   Amazing

You are Amazing!

Amazing people let their light shine bright.

Trace each letter or word. Practice writing each letter on your own.

a   a a a a a a a

a a a a a a a

a

a

amazing amazing

Be amazing!

Amazing people let their light shine bright.

BE AMAZING!

Armadillo

Name:_____ Date:_____

Write a word that begins with the letter below in cursive.. Then, use the word in a sentence writing in cursuive.

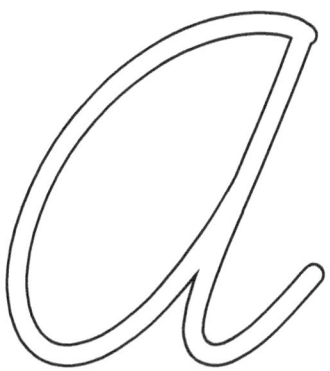

a

1.
2.
3.

Trace each letter or word. Practice writing each letter on your own.

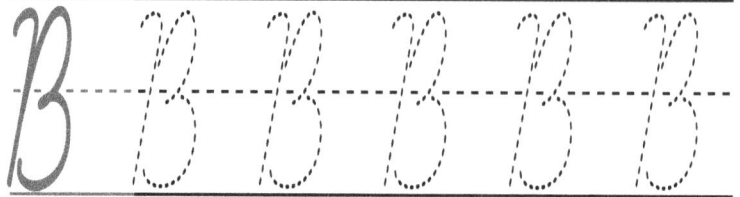

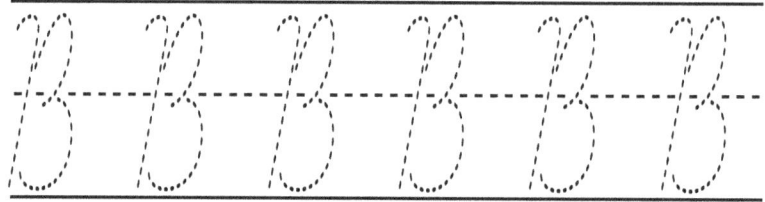

$\mathcal{B}$

$\mathcal{B}$ $\mathcal{B}$ $\mathcal{B}$ $\mathcal{B}$ $\mathcal{B}$ $\mathcal{B}$

$\mathcal{B}$ $\mathcal{B}$ $\mathcal{B}$ $\mathcal{B}$ $\mathcal{B}$ $\mathcal{B}$

$\mathcal{B}$

$\mathcal{B}$

Bold Bold Bold

You are Bold!

Make positive bold and beautiful choices for your life.

Trace each letter or word. Practice writing each letter on your own.

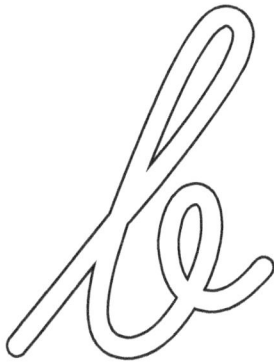

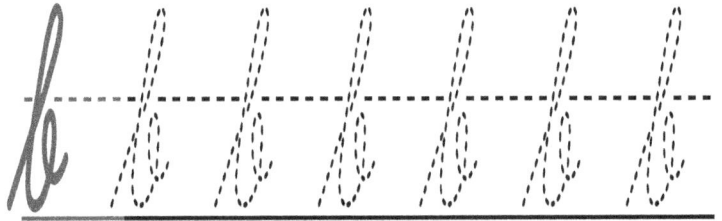

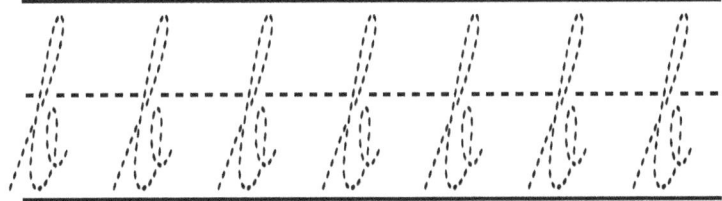

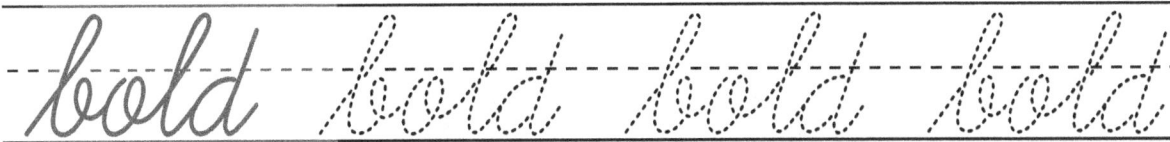

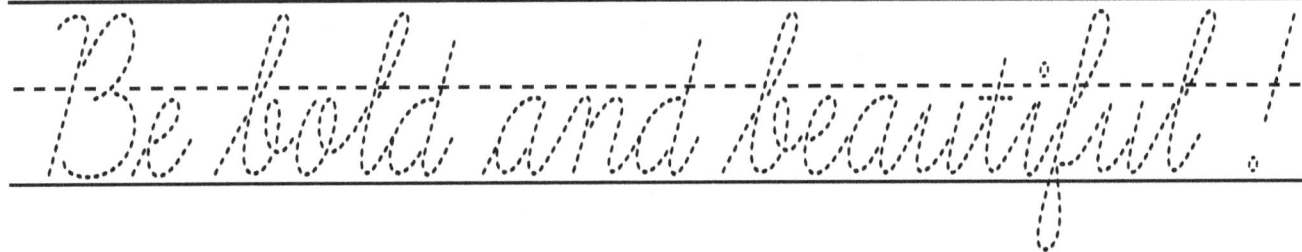

b b b b b b b b

b b b b b b b

b

b

bold bold bold bold

Be bold and beautiful!

Make positive bold and beautiful choices for your life.

you are BOLD!

Butterfly

Name:_____ Date:_____

Write a word that begins with the letter below in cursive. Then, use the word in a sentence writing in cursuive.

$\mathcal{B}$

1. _____

2. _____

3. _____

Trace each letter or word. Practice writing each letter on your own.

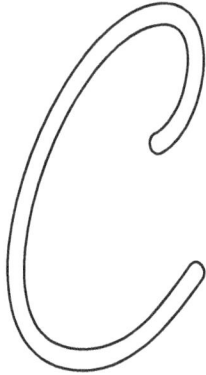

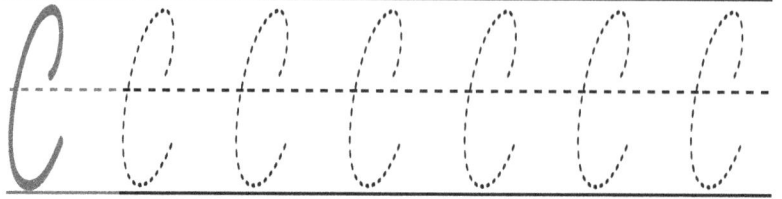

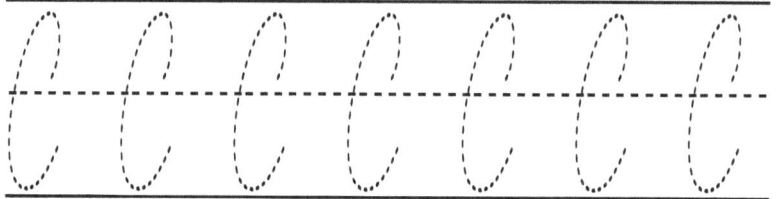

C

C C C C C C C

C C C C C C C

C

C

Courageous Courageous

You are Courageous!

Show that you are courageous by showing who you really are daily.

Trace each letter or word. Practice writing each letter on your own.

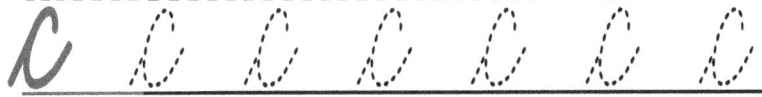

C

c *c* *c* *c* *c* *c* *c*

c *c* *c* *c* *c* *c* *c*

c

c

courageous *courageous*

Be courageous!

Show that you are courageous by showing who you really are daily.

Be Courageous!

Cheetah

Name:_____ Date:_____

Write a word that begins with the letter below in cursive. Then, use the word in a sentence writing in cursuive.

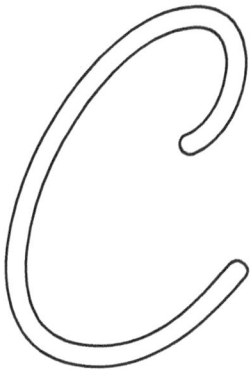

$\mathcal{C}$

1. -

2. -

3. -

Trace each letter or word. Practice writing each letter on your own.

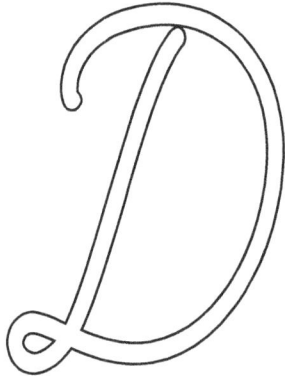

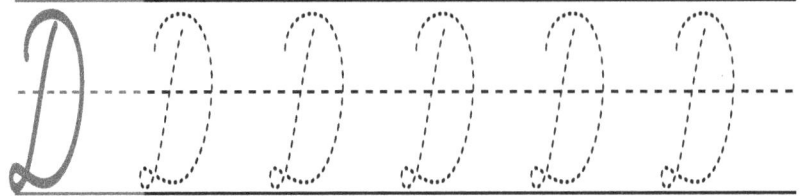

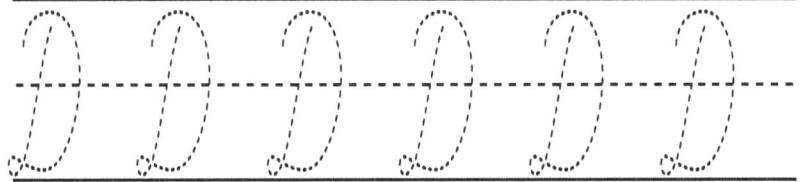

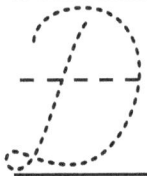

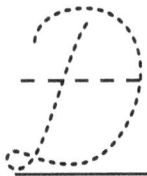

$\mathcal{D}$ $\mathcal{D}$ $\mathcal{D}$ $\mathcal{D}$ $\mathcal{D}$ $\mathcal{D}$ $\mathcal{D}$

$\mathcal{D}$ $\mathcal{D}$ $\mathcal{D}$ $\mathcal{D}$ $\mathcal{D}$ $\mathcal{D}$

$\mathcal{D}$

$\mathcal{D}$

Determined Determined

You are Determined!

Always be determined to learn and to reach for your dreams.

Trace each letter or word. Practice writing each letter on your own.

d   d   d   d   d   d

d   d   d   d   d   d

d

d

determined   determined

Be determined!

Always be determined to learn and to reach for your dreams.

Name:_____ Date:_____

Write a word that begins with the letter below in cursive.. Then, use the word in a sentence writing in cursuive.

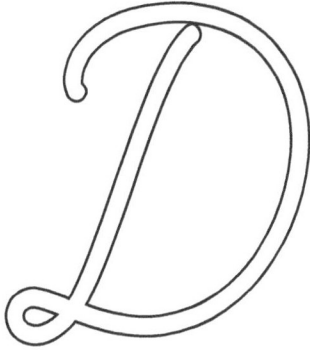

$\mathcal{D}$

1.

2.

3.

Name:_____ Date:_____

Trace each letter or word. Practice writing each letter on your own.

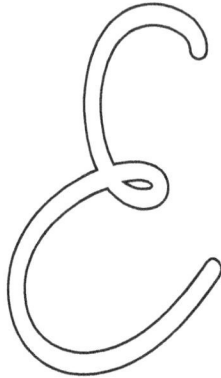

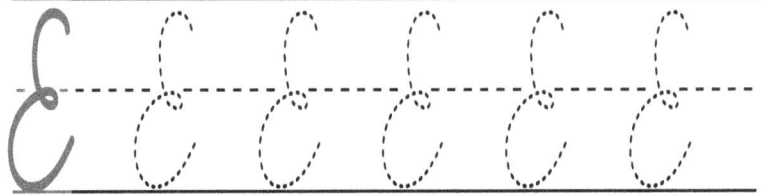

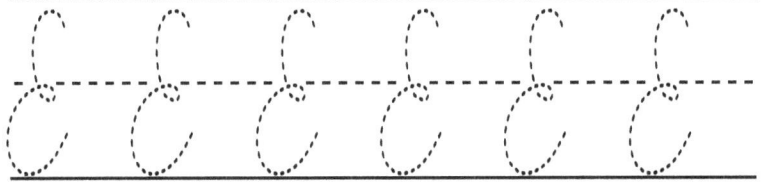

E   E E E E E E
     E E E E E E

E

E

Excellent Excellent

You are Excellent!

Show how excellent you are in everything you do.

Trace each letter or word. Practice writing each letter on your own.

R

R *R* *R* *R* *R* *R*

R *R* *R* *R* *R* *R*

R

R

excellent *excellent*

Be excellent!

Show how excellent you are in everything you do.

Be Excellent!

Eagle

Name:_____ Date:_____

Write a word that begins with the letter below in cursive. Then, use the word in a sentence writing in cursuive.

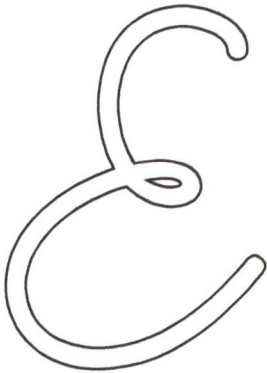

$\mathcal{E}$

1. _____

2. _____

3. _____

Trace each letter or word. Practice writing each letter on your own.

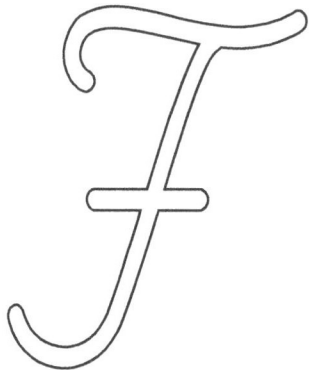

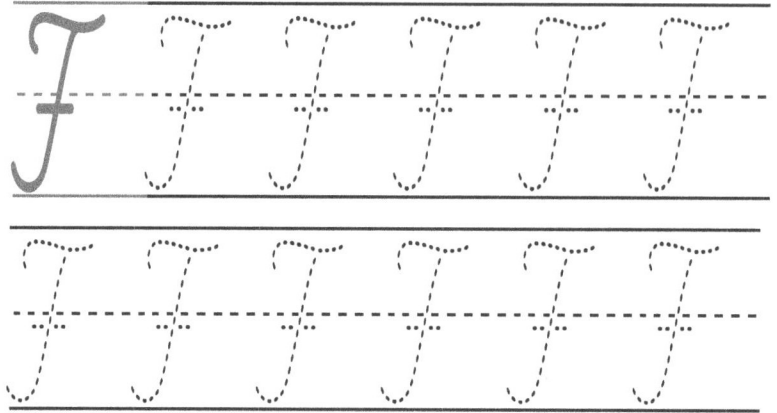

$\mathcal{F}$

$\mathcal{F}$ $\mathcal{F}$ $\mathcal{F}$ $\mathcal{F}$ $\mathcal{F}$ $\mathcal{F}$

$\mathcal{F}$ $\mathcal{F}$ $\mathcal{F}$ $\mathcal{F}$ $\mathcal{F}$ $\mathcal{F}$

$\mathcal{F}$

$\mathcal{F}$

Fantastic Fantastic

You are Fantastic!

Believe that fantastic things will happen in your life.

Trace each letter or word. Practice writing each letter on your own.

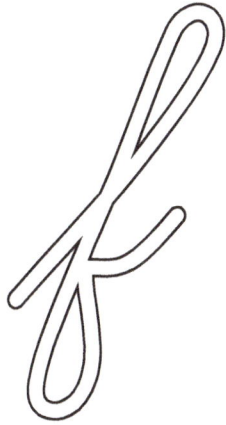

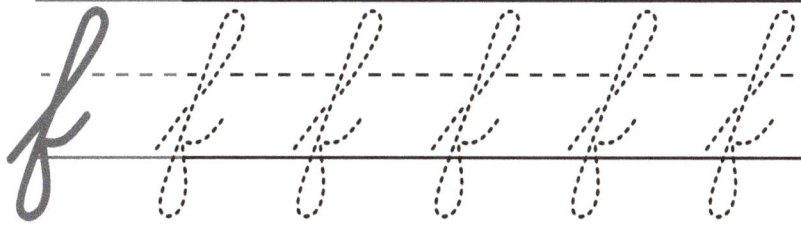

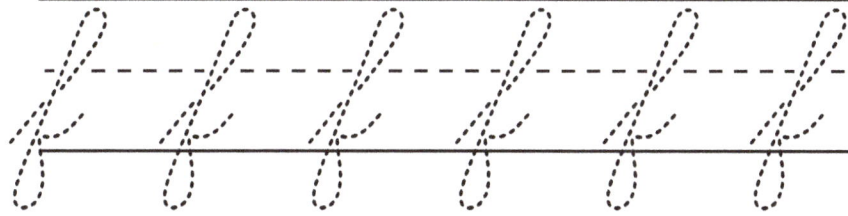

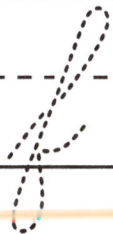

f   *f f f f f f*

f f f f f f

f

f

fantastic fantastic

Be fantastic!

Believe that fantastic things will happen in your life.

YOU ARE FANTASTIC!

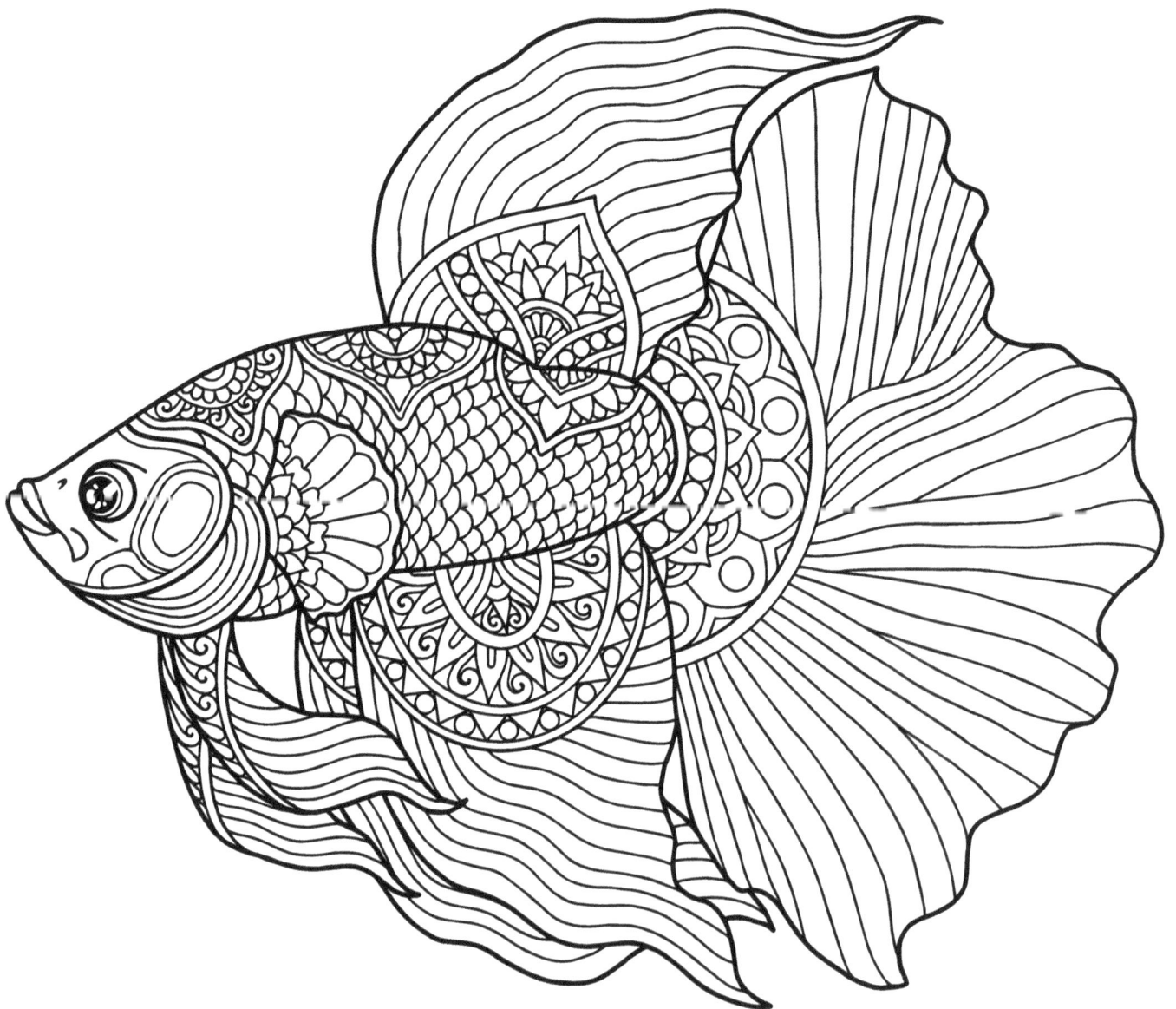

Fish

Name:_____ Date:_____

Write a word that begins with the letter below in cursive. Then, use the word in a sentence writing in cursuive.

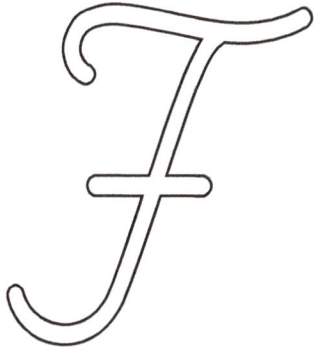

$\mathcal{F}$

1. -

2. -

3. -

- -

- -

- -

- -

Trace each letter or word. Practice writing each letter on your own.

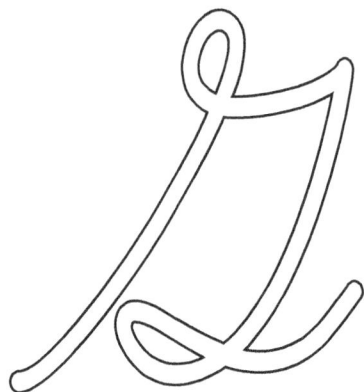

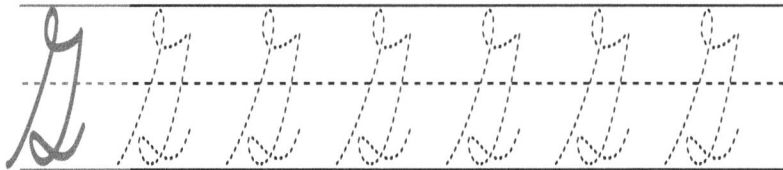

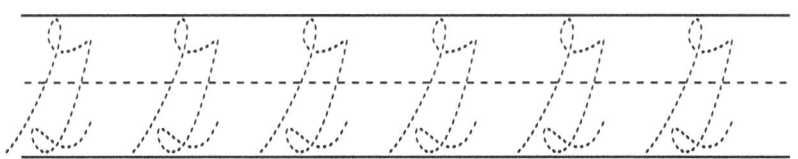

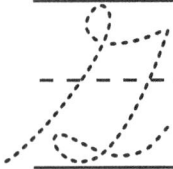

G G G G G G G

G G G G G G

G

G

Gifted Gifted Gifted

You are Gifted!

Everyone has a gift, when you find yours use it to the fullest.

Trace each letter or word. Practice writing each letter on your own.

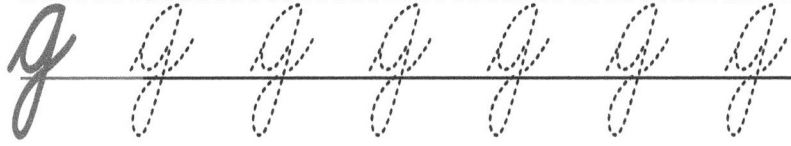

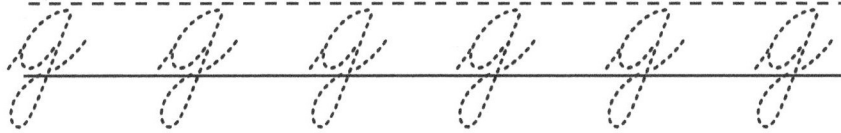

G g g g g g g g

G G G G G G G

g

G

gifted   *gifted*   *gifted*

Be gifted!

Everyone has a gift, when you find yours use it to the fullest.

Be
Gifted!

Giraffe

Name:_____ Date:_____

Write a word that begins with the letter below in cursive. Then, use the word in a sentence writing in cursuive.

1.

2.

3.

Trace each letter or word. Practice writing each letter on your own.

H   H H H H H H

H H H H H H

H

H

Honest Honest Honest

You are Honest!

When you are honest people will trust you more.

Trace each letter or word. Practice writing each letter on your own.

h

h h h h h h

h h h h h h

h

h

honest honest honest

Be honest!

When you are honest people will trust you more.

YOU ARE HONEST!

Horse

Name:_____ Date:_____

Write a word that begins with the letter below in cursive. Then, use the word in a sentence writing in cursuive.

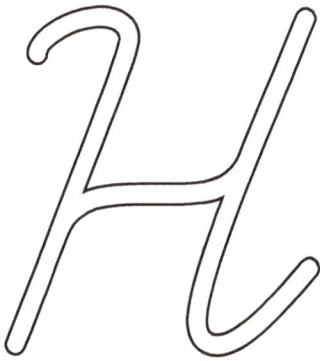

H

1.

2.

3.

Trace each letter or word. Practice writing each letter on your own.

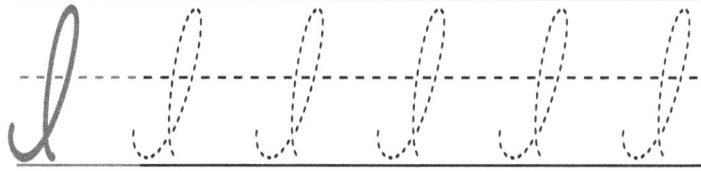

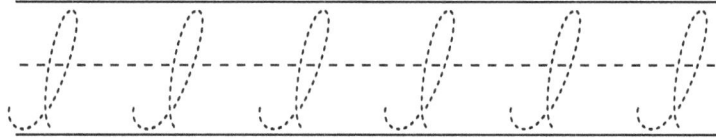

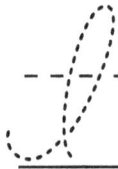

I *I I I I I I*

I I I I I I

I

I

Intelligent Intelligent

You are Intelligent!

Surround yourself with intelligent friends just like you.

Name:_____ Date:_____

Trace each letter or word. Practice writing each letter on your own.

i   *i* *i* *i* *i* *i* *i*

i *i* *i* *i* *i* *i*

i

i

intelligent *intelligent*

Be intelligent!

Surround yourself with intelligent friends just like you.

Be Intelligent!

Iguana

Write a word that begins with the letter below in cursive. Then, use the word in a sentence writing in cursuive.

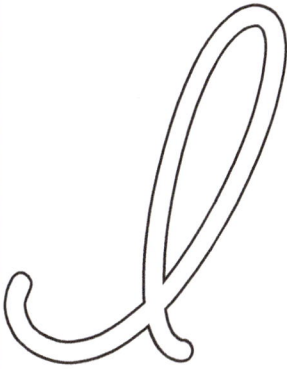

l

1.

2.

3.

Trace each letter or word. Practice writing each letter on your own.

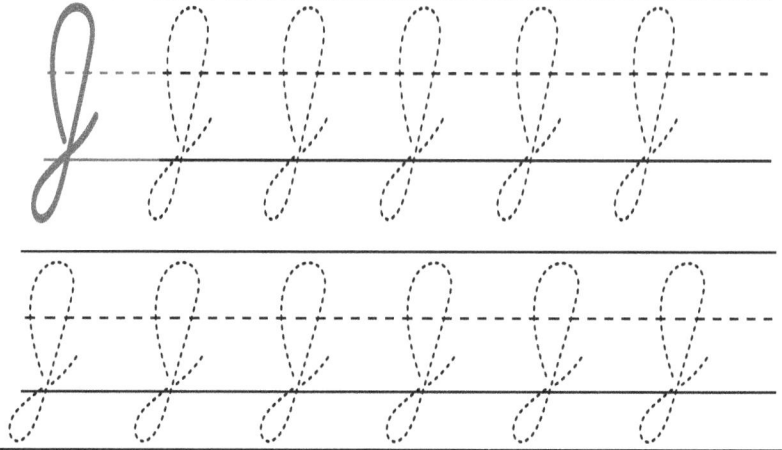

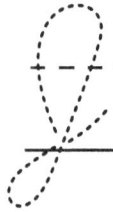

J J J J J J

J J J J J J

J

J

Jewel Jewel Jewel

You are Jewel!

You are a jewel to the world..

Trace each letter or word. Practice writing each letter on your own.

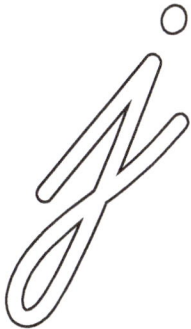

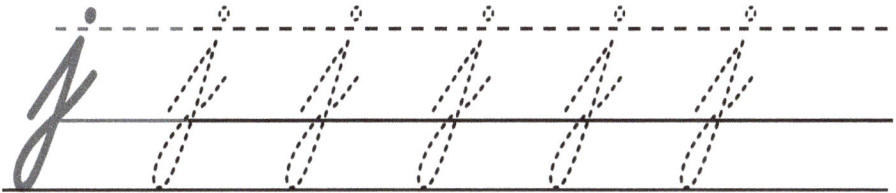

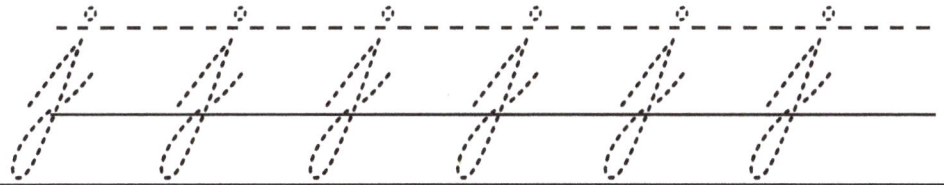

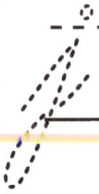

j   j j j j j j

j j j j j j

j

j

jewel   jewel   jewel

Be a jewel!

You are a jewel to the world..

YOU ARE A JEWEL!

Jellyfish

Write a word that begins with the letter below in cursive. Then, use the word in a sentence writing in cursuive.

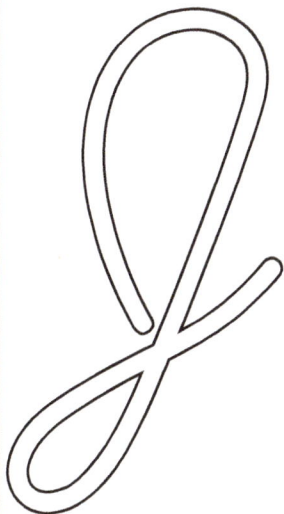

J

1.

2.

3.

Trace each letter or word. Practice writing each letter on your own.

K

K K K K K K

K K K K K K

K

K

Kind Kind Kind

You are Kind!

You are one of a kind and it shows in your acts of kindness.

Name:_____ Date:_____

Trace each letter or word. Practice writing each letter on your own.

k   k   k   k   k   k   k

k   k   k   k   k   k

k

k

kind   kind   kind

Be kind!

You are one of a kind and it shows in your acts of kindness.

BE KIND!

Koala

Name:_____ Date:_____

Write a word that begins with the letter below in cursive. Then, use the word in a sentence writing in cursuive.

$\mathcal{K}$ 1.

       2.

       3.

Trace each letter or word. Practice writing each letter on your own.

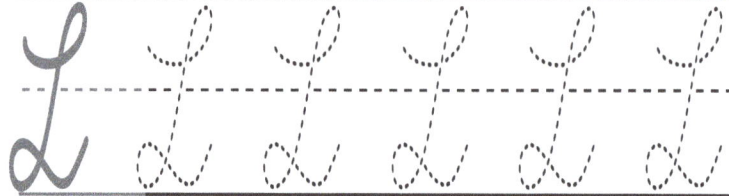

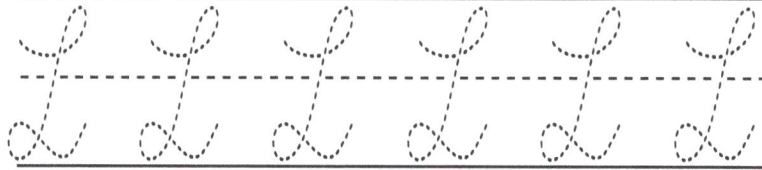

$\mathcal{L}$ $\mathcal{L}$ $\mathcal{L}$ $\mathcal{L}$ $\mathcal{L}$ $\mathcal{L}$ $\mathcal{L}$

$\mathcal{L}$ $\mathcal{L}$ $\mathcal{L}$ $\mathcal{L}$ $\mathcal{L}$ $\mathcal{L}$

$\mathcal{L}$

$\mathcal{L}$

Lovable Lovable

You are Lovable!

You show many admirable and lovable traits.

Trace each letter or word. Practice writing each letter on your own.

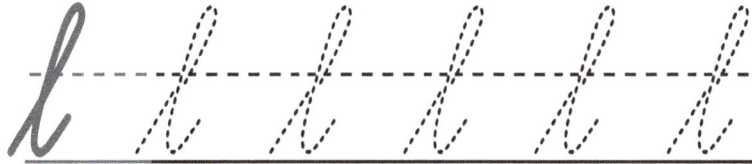

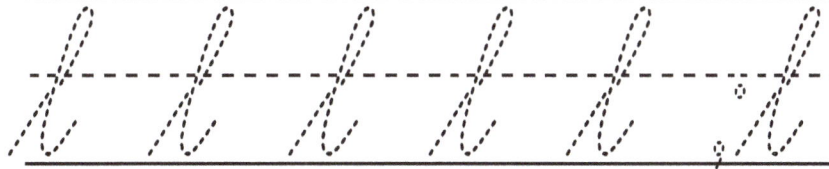

l *l* *l* *l* *l* *l*

l *l* *l* *l* *l* *l*

l

l

lovable *lovable*

Be lovable!

You show many admirable and lovable traits.

You are Lovable!

Lion

Write a word that begins with the letter below in cursive. Then, use the word in a sentence writing in cursuive. .

$\mathcal{L}$

1. _____

2. _____

3. _____

Name:_____ Date:_____

Trace each letter or word. Practice writing each letter on your own.

M   M m m m m m
      m m m m m m

M

M

Magnificent Magnificent

You are Magnificent!

The ideas and dreams you have are magnificent.

Name:_____ Date:_____

Trace each letter or word. Practice writing each letter on your own.

$\mathcal{M}$ $\mathcal{M}$ $\mathcal{M}$ $\mathcal{M}$ $\mathcal{M}$ $\mathcal{M}$ $\mathcal{M}$

m m m m m m m

m

m

$magnificent$ $magnificent$

Be $magnificent$ $!$

The ideas and dreams you have are magnificent.

BE MAGNIFICENT!

Monkey

Write a word that begins with the letter below in cursive. Then, use the word in a sentence writing in cursuive.

m

1. _____

2. _____

3. _____

_____

_____

_____

_____

Trace each letter or word. Practice writing each letter on your own.

n *n* *n* *n* *n* *n*

n *n* *n* *n* *n* *n*

n

n

Noble *Noble* *Noble*

You are Noble!

People are inspired by your noble acts of kindness.

Name:_____ Date:_____

Trace each letter or word. Practice writing each letter on your own.

n   *n n n n n n n*

n n n n n n n

m

m

noble noble noble noble

Be noble!

People are inspired by your noble acts of kindness.

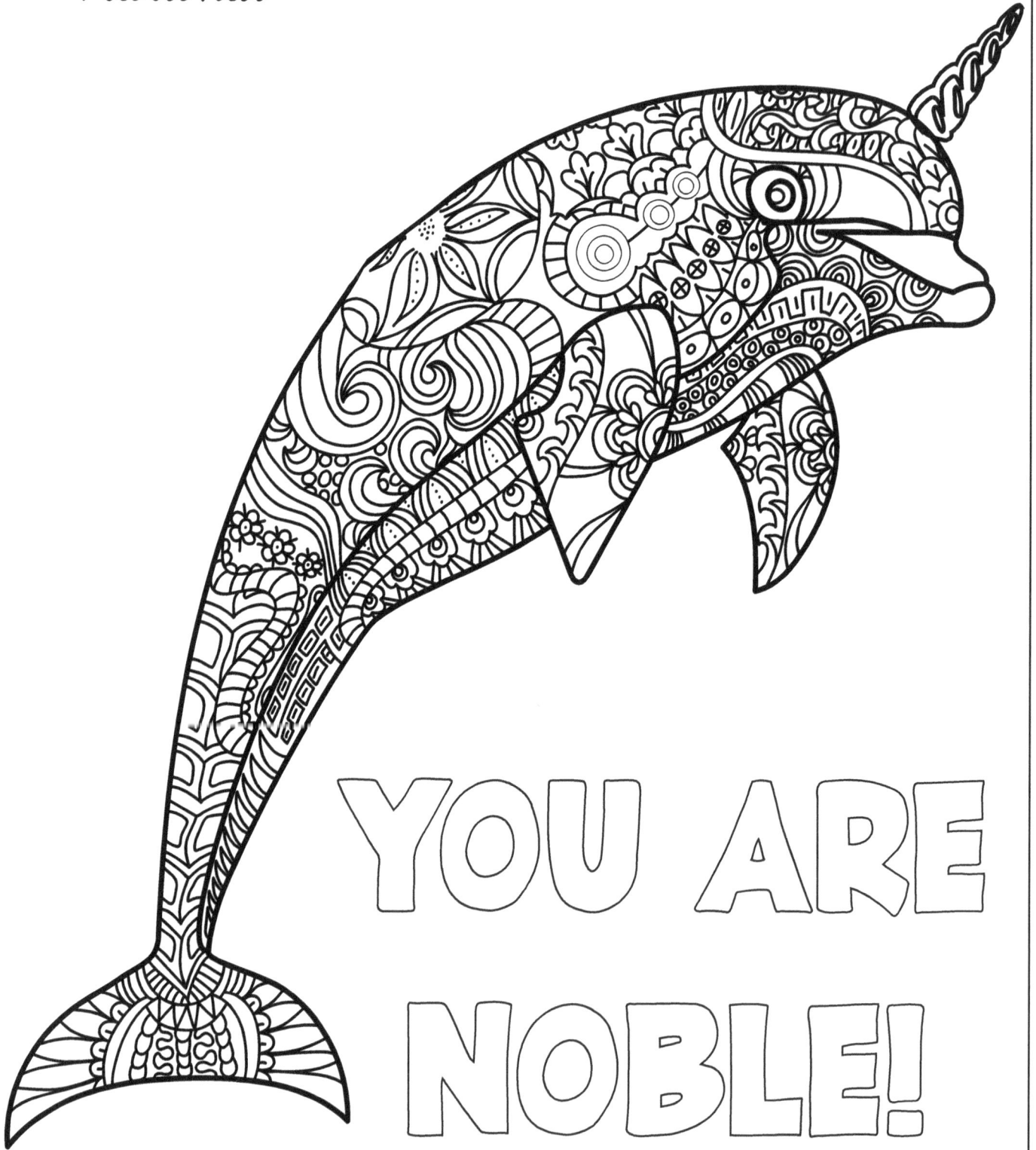

Narwhal

YOU ARE NOBLE!

Write a word that begins with the letter below in cursive. Then, use the word in a sentence writing in cursuive.

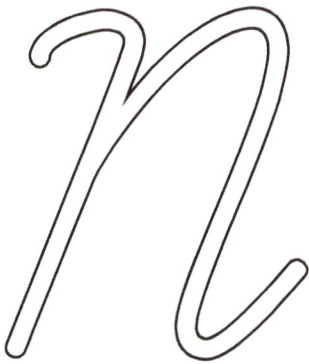

n

1. _____

2. _____

3. _____

Name:_____ Date:_____

Trace each letter or word. Practice writing each letter on your own.

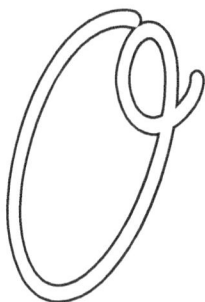

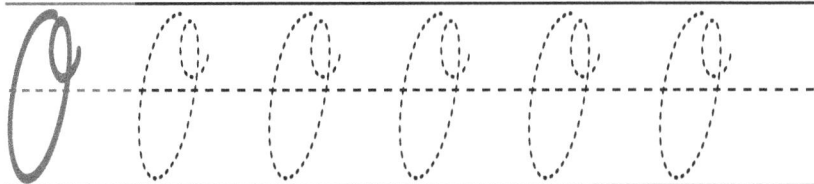

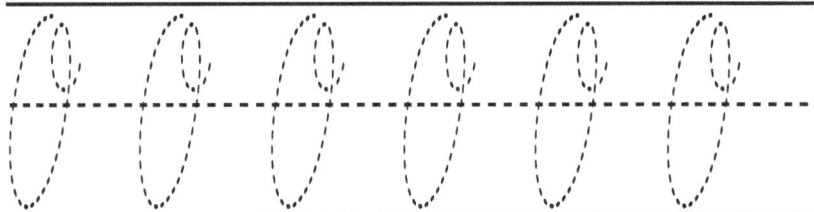

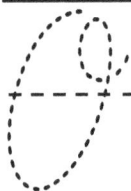

O

O O O O O O O

O O O O O O O O

O

O

Original Original

You are Original!

Your style is original.

Trace each letter or word. Practice writing each letter on your own.

O

o o o o o o o

o o o o o o o

o

o

original original original

Be original!

Your style is original.

BE ORIGINAL!

Owl

Name:_____ Date:_____

Write a word that begins with the letter below in cursive. Then, use the word in a sentence writing in cursuive.

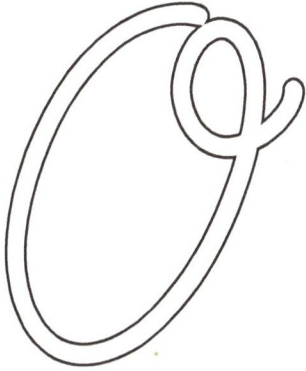

$\mathcal{O}$

1. _____

2. _____

3. _____

Trace each letter or word. Practice writing each letter on your own.

p

p p p p p p p

p p p p p p p

P

P

Powerful Powerful

You are Powerful!

The more you learn, the more powerful you will become.

Trace each letter or word. Practice writing each letter on your own.

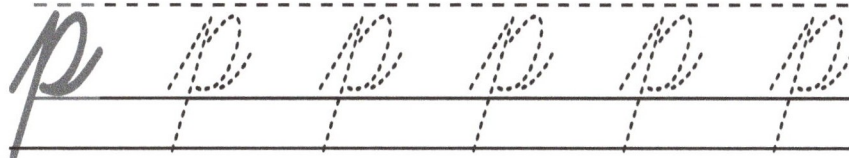

p   p p p p p p p

p p p p p p

p

p

powerful powerful

Be powerful!

The more you learn, the more powerful you will become.

YOU ARE POWERFUL!

Peacock

Name:_____ Date:_____

Write a word that begins with the letter below in cursive. Then, use the word in a sentence writing in cursive.

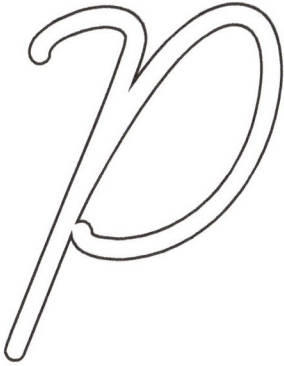

$\mathcal{P}$

1. --

2. --

3. --

Trace each letter or word. Practice writing each letter on your own.

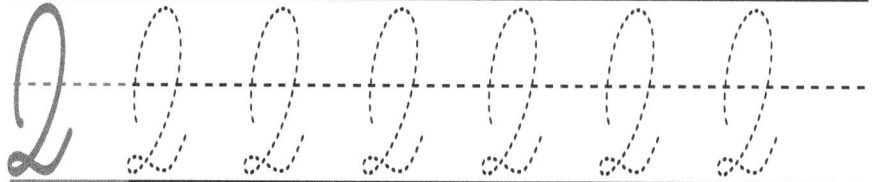

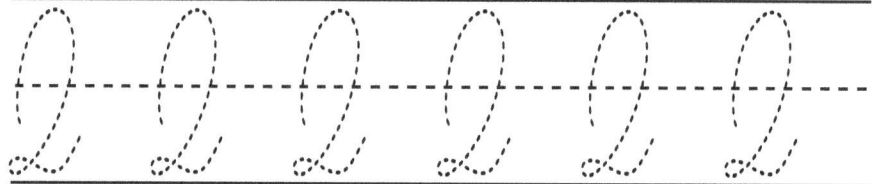

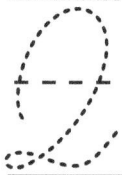

Q

Q Q Q Q Q Q Q

Q Q Q Q Q Q

Q

Q

Quintessential Quintessential

You are Quintessential!

You are a quintessential hero to someone special.

Trace each letter or word. Practice writing each letter on your own.

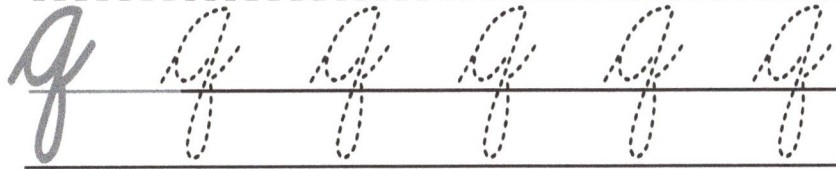

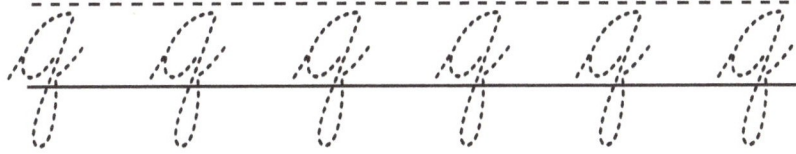

q q q q q q q

q q q q q q

q

q

quintessential quintessential

Be quintessential!

You are a quintessential hero to someone special.

Be Quintessential!

Quokka

Name:_____ Date:_____

Write a word that begins with the letter below in cursive.. Then, use the word in a sentence writing in cursuive.

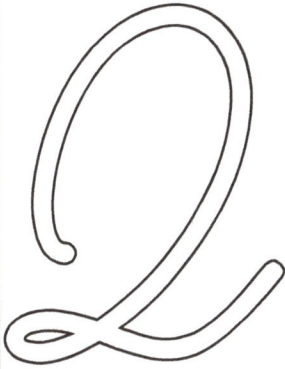

Q

1. -

2. -

3. -

Name:_____ Date:_____

Trace each letter or word. Practice writing each letter on your own.

R

R R R R R R R

R R R R R R

R

R

Respectful Respectful

You are Respectful !

Being respectful will lead to endless possibilites.

Trace each letter or word. Practice writing each letter on your own.

n   *n n n n n n n*

n n n n n n n

n

n

respectful respectful respectful

Be respectful !

Being respectful will lead to endless possibilites.

YOU ARE RESPECTFUL!

Rabbit

Name:_____ Date:_____

Write a word that begins with the letter below in cursive.. Then, use the word in a sentence writing in cursuive. .

$\mathcal{R}$

1. --

2. --

3. --

Name:_____ Date:_____

Trace each letter or word. Practice writing each letter on your own.

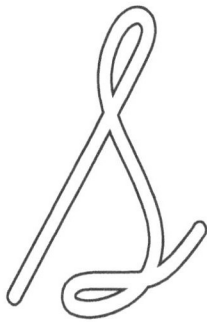

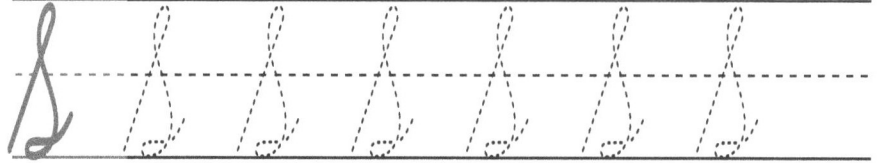

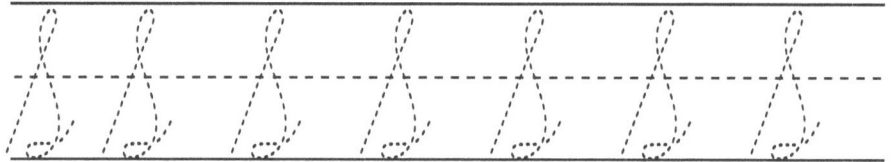

S

Special *Special* *Special*

You are Special !

Your spirit is a special kind of spirit.

Trace each letter or word. Practice writing each letter on your own.

s *s* *s* *s* *s* *s* *s*

s *s* *s* *s* *s* *s* *s*

s

s

special *special* *special* *special*

Be special!

Your spirit is a special kind of spirit.

Be Special!

Seahorse

Name:_____ Date:_____

Write a word that begins with the letter below in cursive. Then, use the word in a sentence writing in cursuive. .

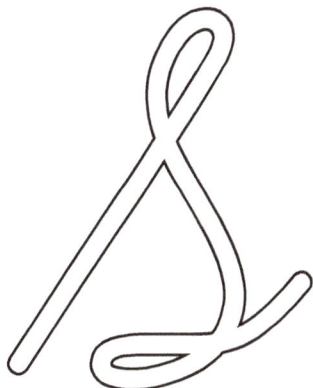

S

1. _____

2. _____

3. _____

Name:_____ Date:_____

Trace each letter or word. Practice writing each letter on your own.

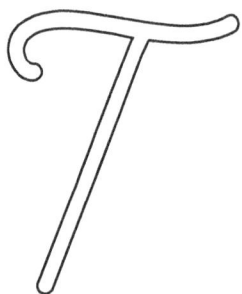

T T T T T T T T

T T T T T T T

T

T

Talented *Talented* *Talented*

You are Talented!

Let your talent lead you to living out your dreams.

Name:_____ Date:_____

Trace each letter or word. Practice writing each letter on your own.

t   t t t t t t t

t t t t t t t

t

t

talented talented talented talented

Be talented!

Let your talent lead you to living out your dreams.

YOU ARE TALENTED!

Tiger

Name:_____ Date:_____

Write a word that begins with the letter below in cursive.. Then, use the word in a sentence writing in cursuive.

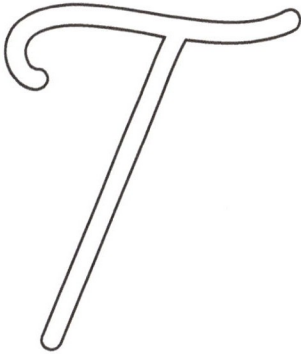

$\mathcal{T}$

1.

2.

3.

Trace each letter or word. Practice writing each letter on your own.

$\mathcal{U}$

$\mathcal{U}$ $\mathcal{U}$ $\mathcal{U}$ $\mathcal{U}$ $\mathcal{U}$ $\mathcal{U}$ $\mathcal{U}$

$\mathcal{U}$ $\mathcal{U}$ $\mathcal{U}$ $\mathcal{U}$ $\mathcal{U}$ $\mathcal{U}$ $\mathcal{U}$

$\mathcal{U}$

$\mathcal{U}$

Unique Unique Unique

You are Unique!

Your life is unique, live your own journey in your way.

Name:_____ Date:_____

Trace each letter or word. Practice writing each letter on your own.

U   U   U   U   U   U   U   U

U   U   U   U   U   U   U

U

U

unique   unique   unique   unique

Be unique!

Your life is unique, live your own journey in your way.

BE UNIQUE!

Ulysses Butterfly

Write a word that begins with the letter below in cursive.. Then, use the word in a sentence writing in cursuive.

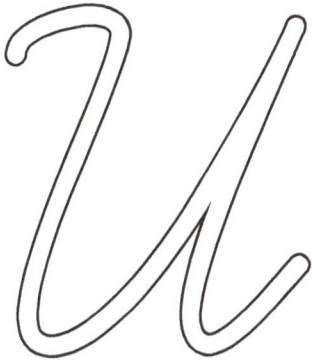

$\mathcal{U}$

1. -

2. -

3. -

- -

- -

- -

Trace each letter or word. Practice writing each letter on your own.

V V V V V V V V V V

V V V V V V V V V

v

v

Victorious Victorious Victorious

You are Victorious!

You will be victorious in everything you do.

Trace each letter or word. Practice writing each letter on your own.

N *N* *N* *N* *N* *N* *N*

N *N* *N* *N* *N* *N* *N*

N

N

victorious *victorious* *victorious*

Be victorious!

You will be victorious in everything you do.

YOU ARE VICTORIOUS!

Vulture

Name:_____ Date:_____

Write a word that begins with the letter below in cursive. Then, use the word in a sentence writing in cursuive.

$\mathcal{V}$

1. -

2. -

3. -

Name:_____ Date:_____

Trace each letter or word. Practice writing each letter on your own.

W

W W W W W W W

W W W W W W W

W

W

Witty Witty Witty Witty Witty

You are Witty!

Show off your witty and charming personality.

Trace each letter or word. Practice writing each letter on your own.

w *w* *w* *w* *w* *w* *w*

w *w* *w* *w* *w* *w* *w*

w

w

witty *witty* *witty* *witty* *witty*

Be witty!

Show off your witty and charming personality.

Be witty!

Wolf

Name:_____ Date:_____

Write a word that begins with the letter below in cursive.. Then, use the word in a sentence writing in cursuive.

$\mathcal{W}$

1. -

2. -

3. -

- -

- -

- -

- -

Trace each letter or word. Practice writing each letter on your own.

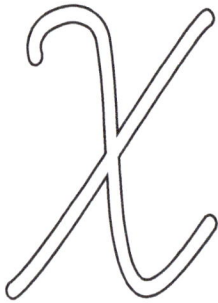

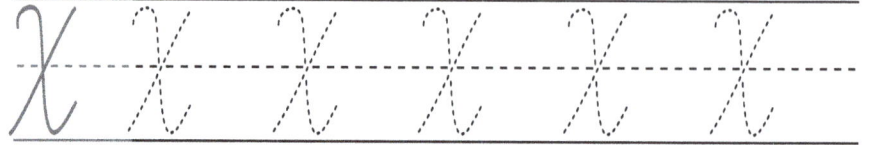

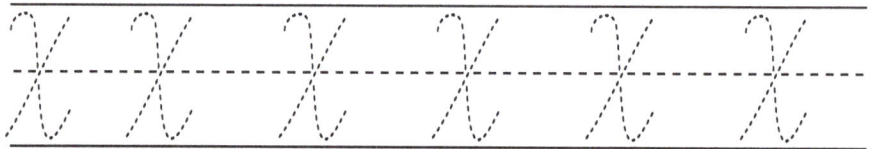

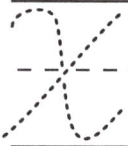

X *X* *X* *X* *X* *X*

X *X* *X* *X* *X* *X*

x

x

X-factor *X-factor* *X-factor*

You are a X-factor!

You have that X-factor that makes you extraordinary.

Name:_____ Date:_____

Trace each letter or word. Practice writing each letter on your own.

x

x x x x x x

x x x x x x

x

x

x-factor   x-factor   x-factor

Be the x-factor!

You have that X-factor that makes you extraordinary.

You are the X-Factor!

Xenops

Write a word that begins with the letter below in cursive.. Then, use the word in a sentence writing in cursuive.

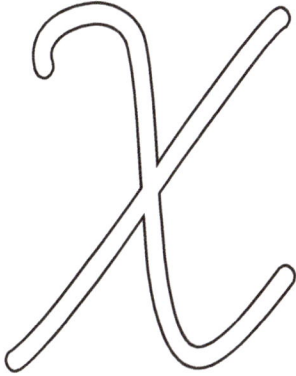

$\mathcal{X}$

1.
2.
3.

Trace each letter or word. Practice writing each letter on your own.

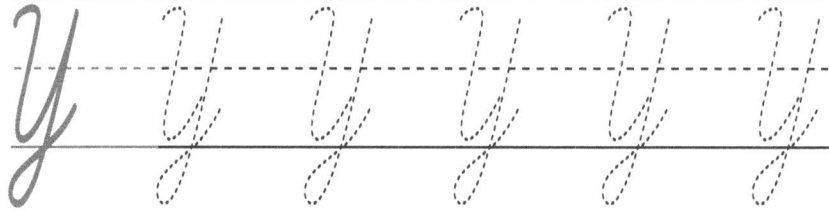

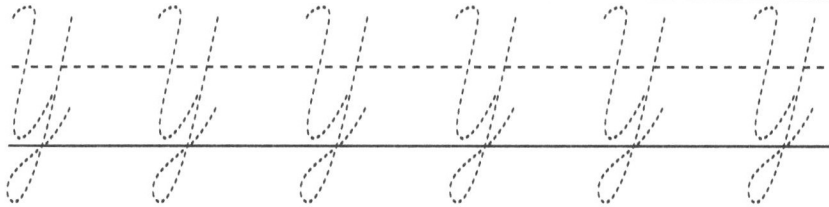

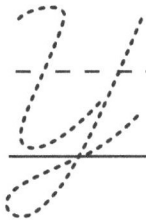

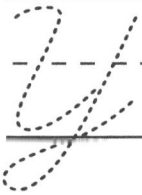

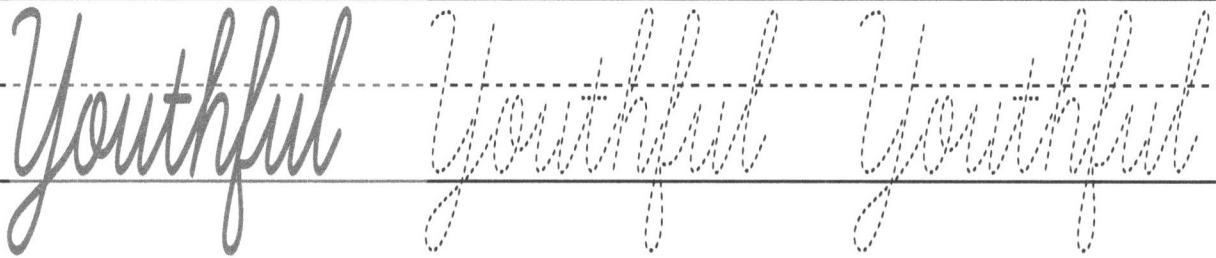

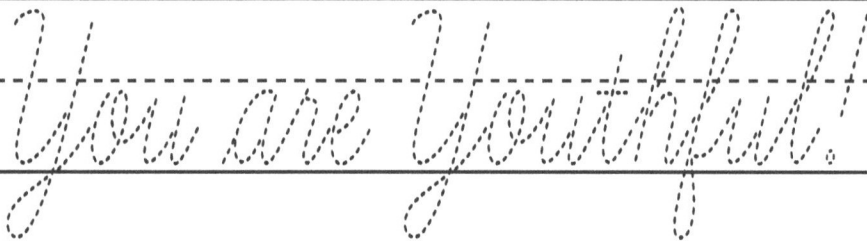

Y

Y Y Y Y Y Y

Y Y Y Y Y Y

Y

Y

Youthful Youthful Youthful

You are Youthful!

Let your youthful side live on forever.

Trace each letter or word. Practice writing each letter on your own.

Y   *Y Y Y Y Y Y Y*

y y y y y y y

Y

Y

youthful youthful youthful

Be youthful!

Let your youthful side live on forever.

Be Youthful

Yak

Name:_____ Date:_____

Write a word that begins with the letter below in cursive. Then, use the word in a sentence writing in cursuive.

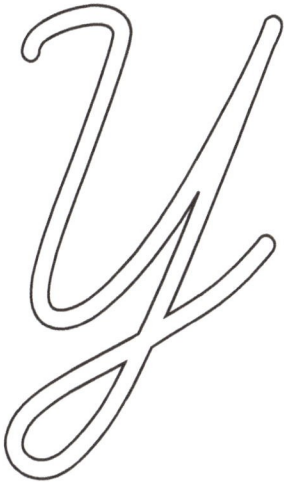

Y

1. -

2. -

3. -

- -

- -

- -

- -

Name:_____ Date:_____

Trace each letter or word. Practice writing each letter on your own.

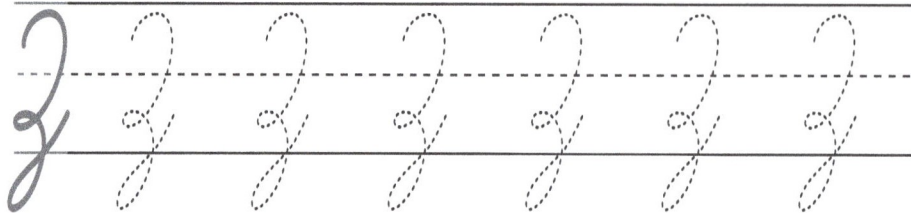

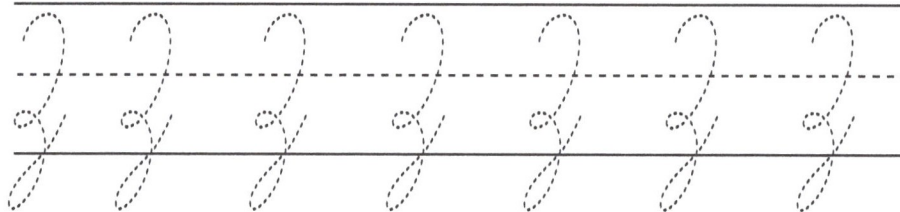

$\mathcal{Z}$

$\mathcal{Z}$ $\mathcal{Z}$ $\mathcal{Z}$ $\mathcal{Z}$ $\mathcal{Z}$ $\mathcal{Z}$ $\mathcal{Z}$

$\mathcal{Z}$ $\mathcal{Z}$ $\mathcal{Z}$ $\mathcal{Z}$ $\mathcal{Z}$ $\mathcal{Z}$ $\mathcal{Z}$

$\mathcal{Z}$

$\mathcal{Z}$

Zestful Zestful Zestful

You are Zestful!

Your zestful personality charms all whom cross your path.

Trace each letter or word. Practice writing each letter on your own.

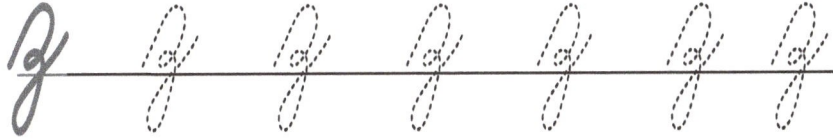

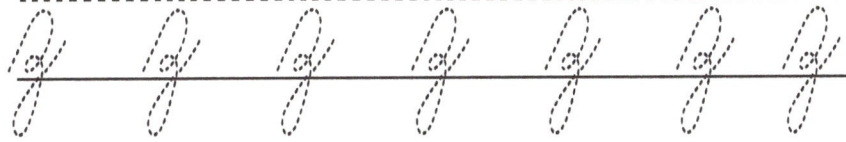

G *G* *G* *G* *G* *G* *G*

g *g* *g* *g* *g* *g* *g*

G

G

zestful *zestful* *zestful* *zestful* *zestful*

You are zestful!

Your zestful personality charms all whom cross your path.

You are Zestful!

Zebra

Write a word that begins with the letter below in cursive. Then, use the word in a sentence writing in cursuive.

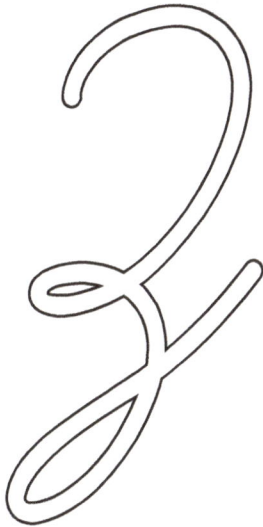

$\mathcal{Z}$

1.

2.

3.

Extra Handwriting Practice Sheets

Name:_____ Date:_____

Trace each letter. Practice writing each letter on your own.

a a a a a a

a a a a

a a a

a a

a

Name:_____ Date:_____

Trace each letter. Practice writing each letter on your own.

a *a* *a* *a* *a* *a*

a *a* *a* *a*

a *a* *a*

a *a*

a

Name:_____ Date:_____

Trace each letter. Practice writing each letter on your own.

$\mathcal{B}$ $\mathcal{B}$ $\mathcal{B}$ $\mathcal{B}$ $\mathcal{B}$ $\mathcal{B}$

$\mathcal{B}$ $\mathcal{B}$ $\mathcal{B}$ $\mathcal{B}$

$\mathcal{B}$ $\mathcal{B}$ $\mathcal{B}$

$\mathcal{B}$ $\mathcal{B}$

$\mathcal{B}$

Name:_____ Date:_____

Trace each letter. Practice writing each letter on your own.

b b b b b b

b b b b

b b b

b b

b

Name:_____ Date:_____

Trace each letter. Practice writing each letter on your own.

C C C C C C

e e e e

e e e

e e

e

Trace each letter. Practice writing each letter on your own.

Name:_____ Date:_____

Trace each letter. Practice writing each letter on your own.

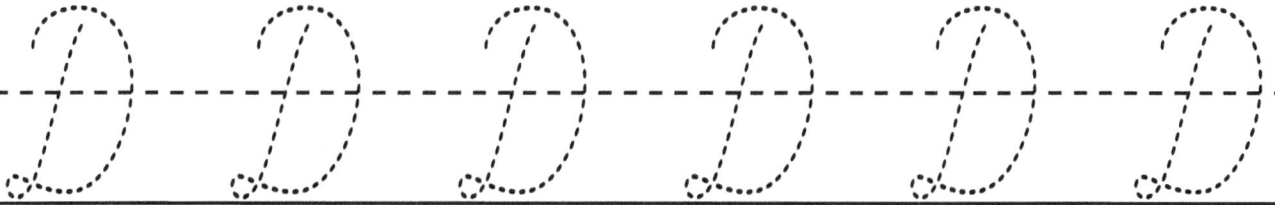

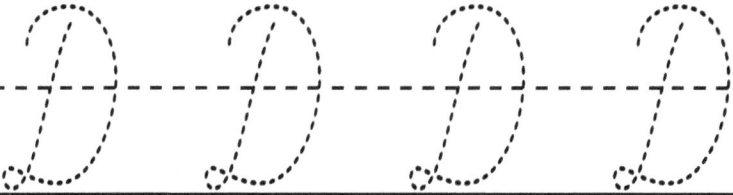

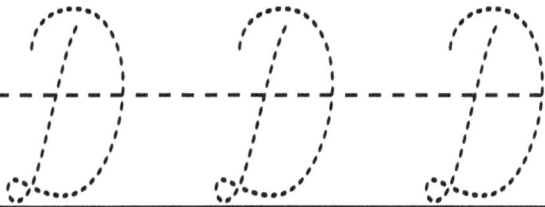

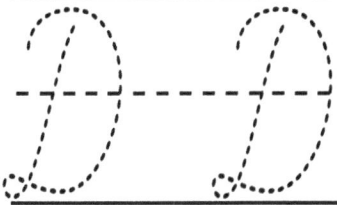

$\mathcal{D}$ $\mathcal{D}$ $\mathcal{D}$ $\mathcal{D}$ $\mathcal{D}$ $\mathcal{D}$

$\mathcal{D}$ $\mathcal{D}$ $\mathcal{D}$ $\mathcal{D}$

$\mathcal{D}$ $\mathcal{D}$ $\mathcal{D}$

$\mathcal{D}$ $\mathcal{D}$

$\mathcal{D}$

Trace each letter. Practice writing each letter on your own.

d d d d d d d

d d d d

d d d

d d

d

Name:_____ Date:_____

Trace each letter. Practice writing each letter on your own.

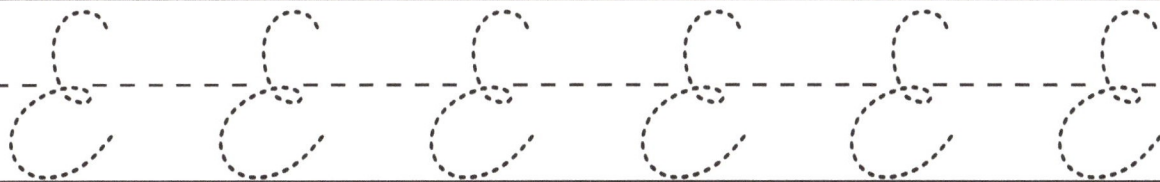

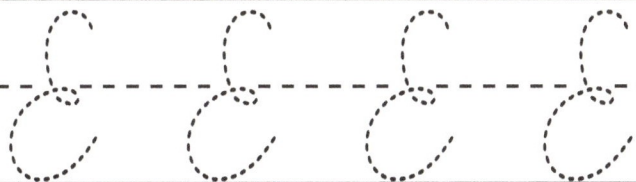

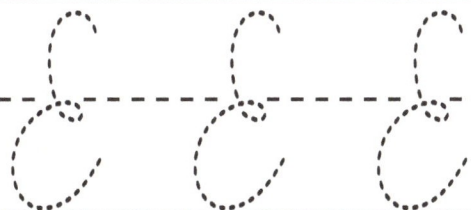

E E E E E E

E E E E

E E E

E E

E

Name:_____ Date:_____

Trace each letter. Practice writing each letter on your own.

Trace each letter. Practice writing each letter on your own.

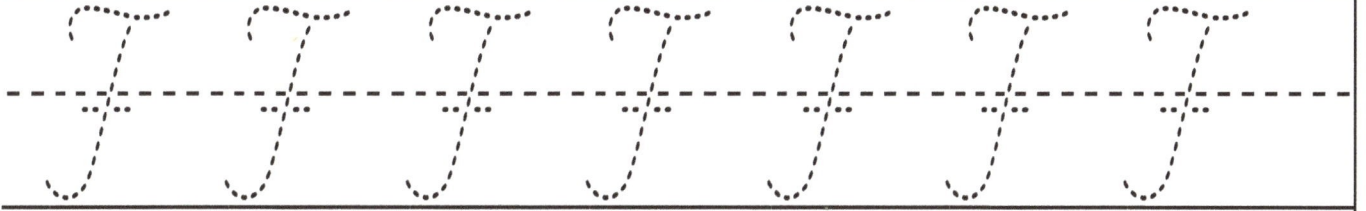

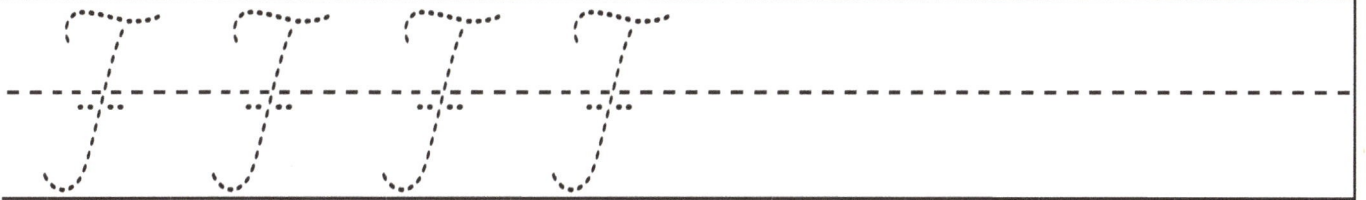

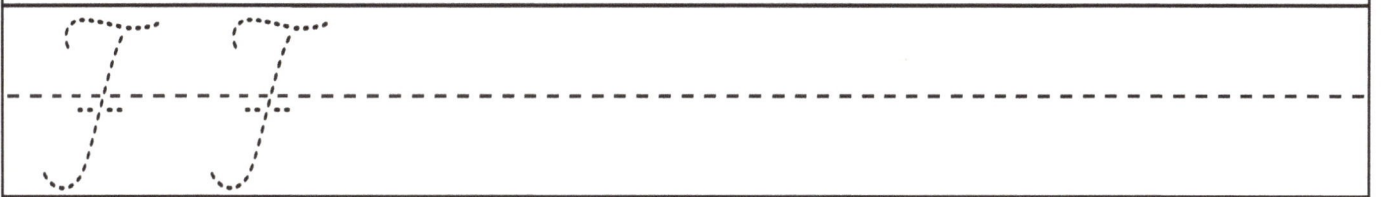

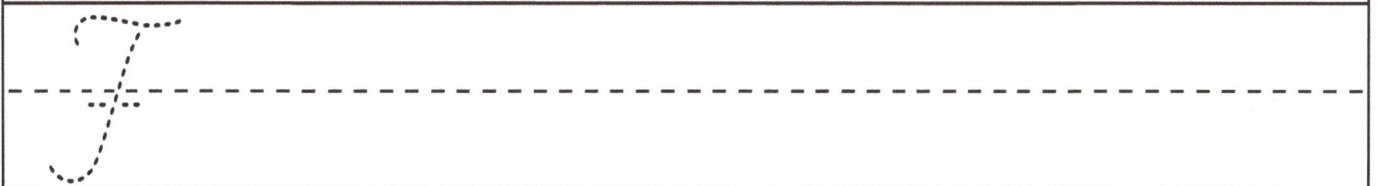

$\mathcal{F}$ $\mathcal{F}$ $\mathcal{F}$ $\mathcal{F}$ $\mathcal{F}$ $\mathcal{F}$ $\mathcal{F}$

$\mathcal{F}$ $\mathcal{F}$ $\mathcal{F}$ $\mathcal{F}$

$\mathcal{F}$ $\mathcal{F}$ $\mathcal{F}$

$\mathcal{F}$ $\mathcal{F}$

$\mathcal{F}$

Trace each letter. Practice writing each letter on your own.

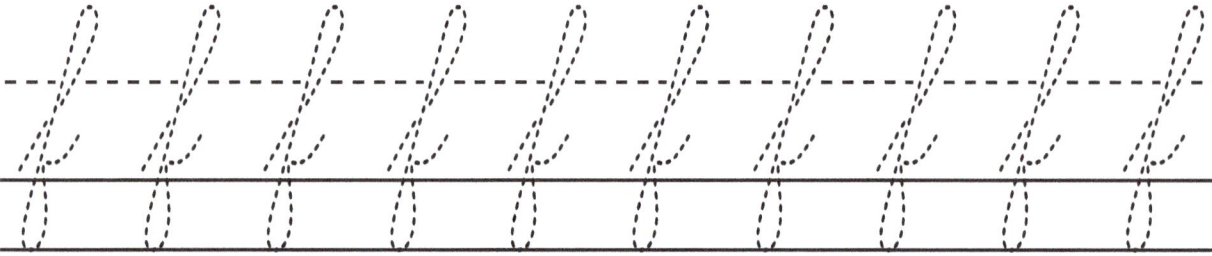

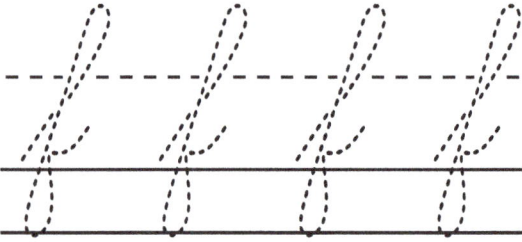

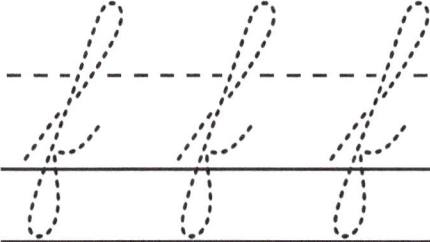

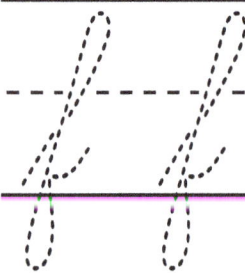

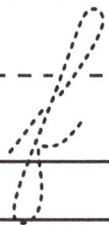

f f f f f f f f f f

f f f f

f f f

f f

f

Name:_____ Date:_____

Trace each letter. Practice writing each letter on your own.

Trace each letter. Practice writing each letter on your own.

G G G G G G G G G

G G G G

G G G

G G

G

Trace each letter. Practice writing each letter on your own.

H H H H H H H H

H H H H

H H H

H H

H

Trace each letter. Practice writing each letter on your own.

h h h h h h h h h h h

h h h h

h h h

h h

h

Trace each letter. Practice writing each letter on your own.

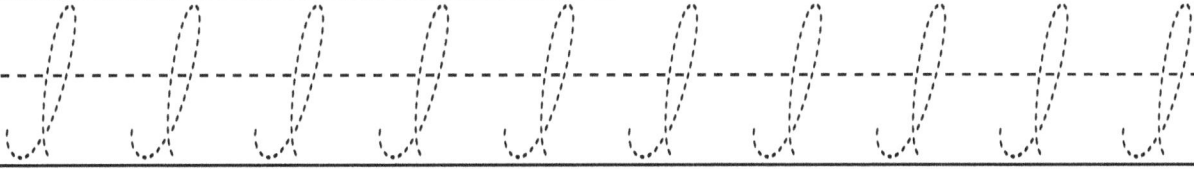

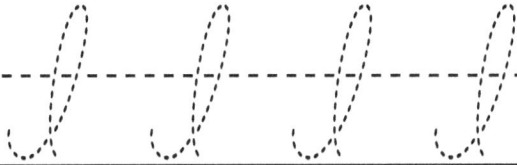

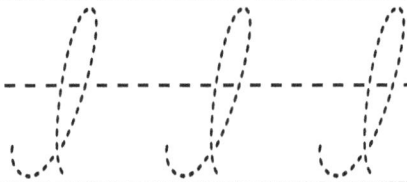

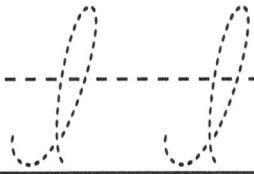

l l l l l l l l l l

l l l l

l l l

l l

l

Trace each letter. Practice writing each letter on your own.

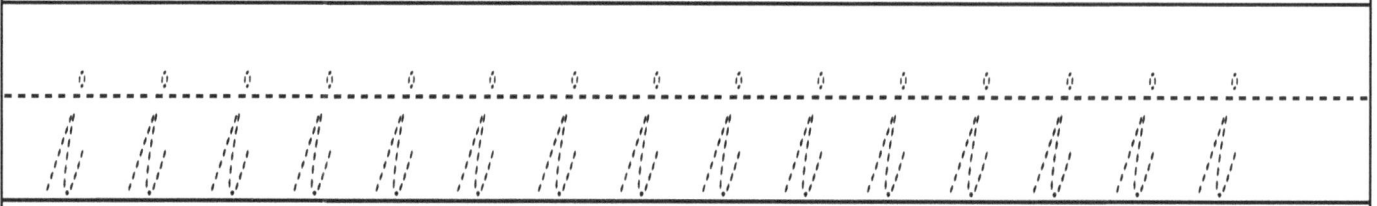

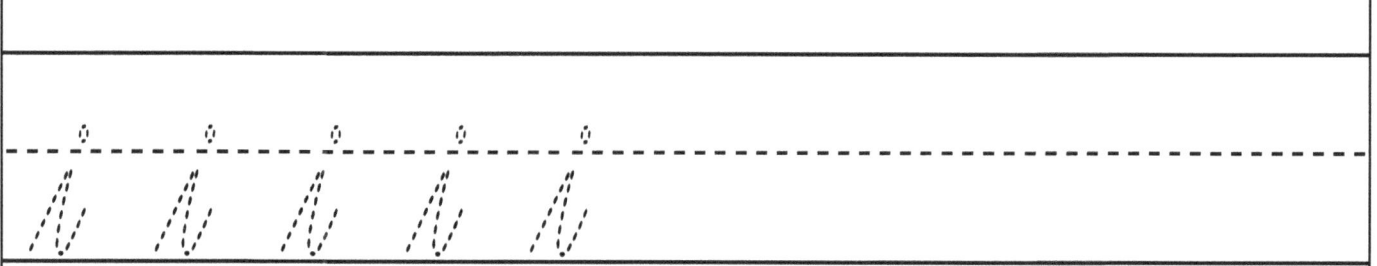

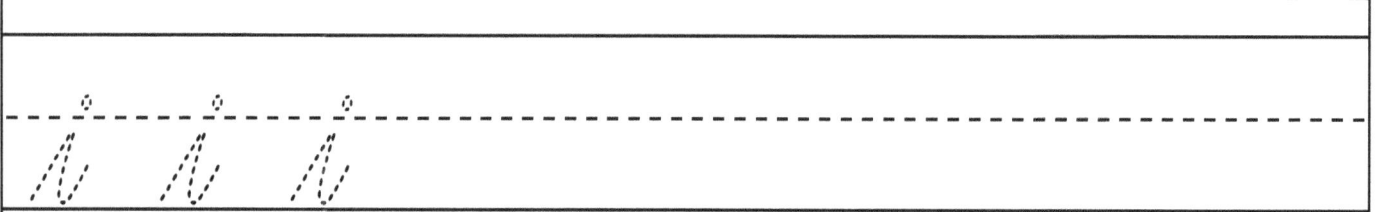

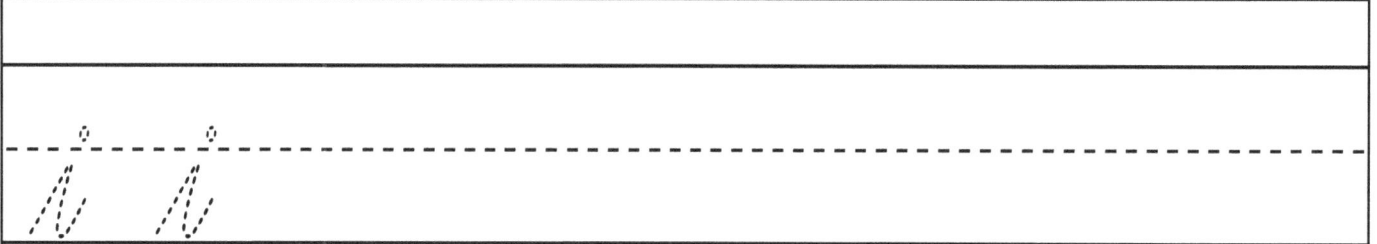

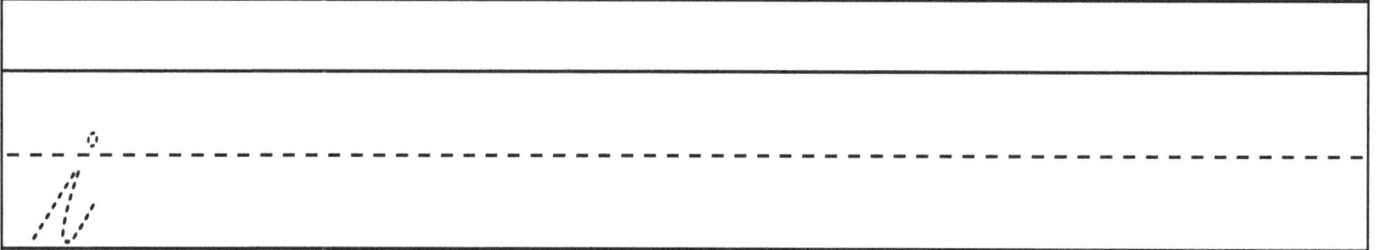

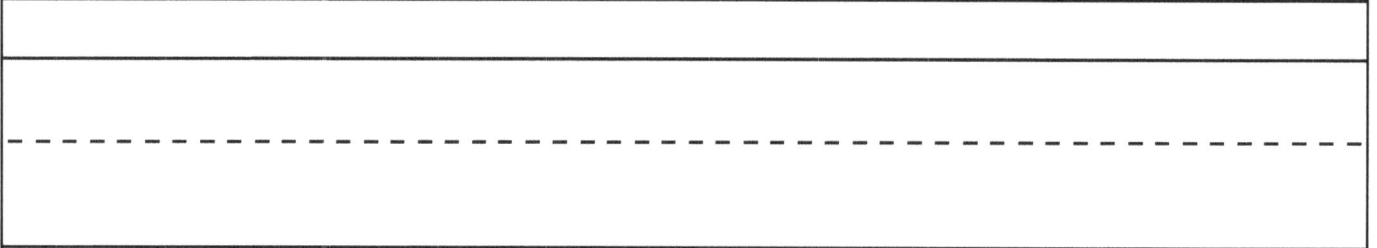

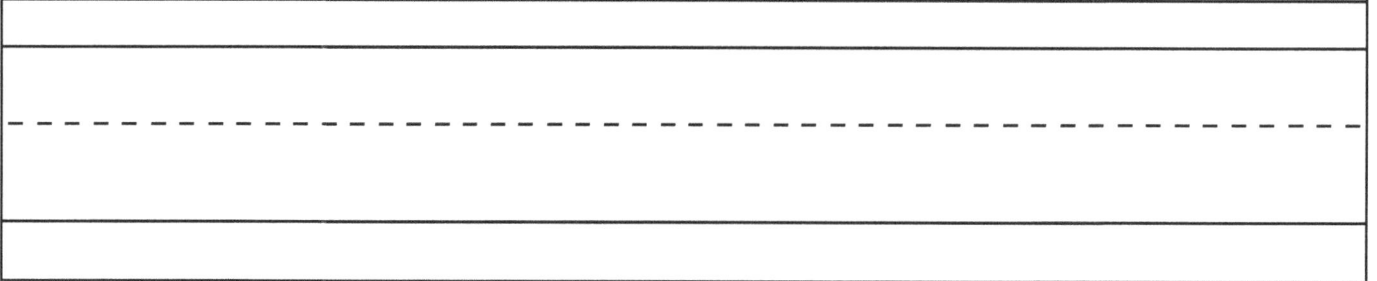

Trace each letter. Practice writing each letter on your own.

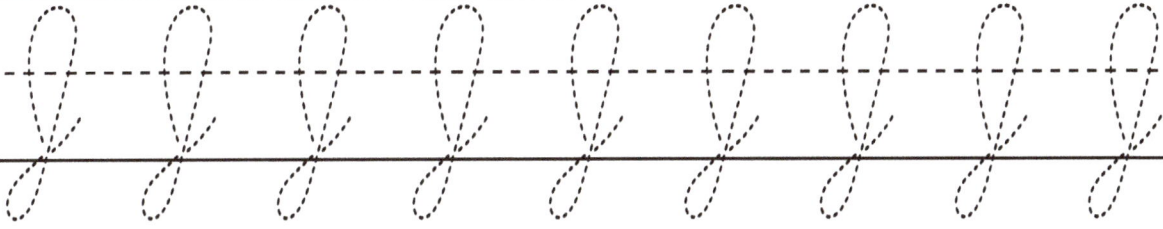

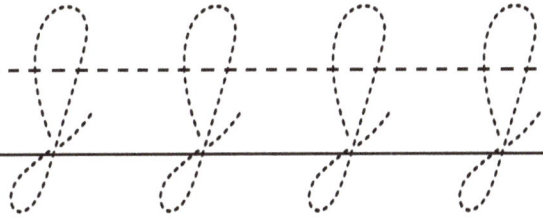

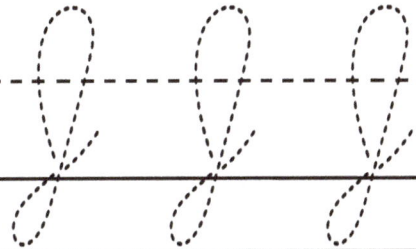

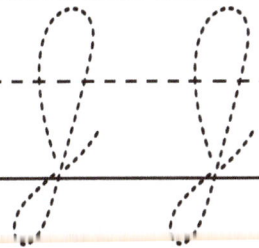

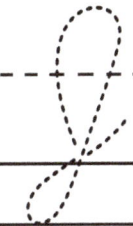

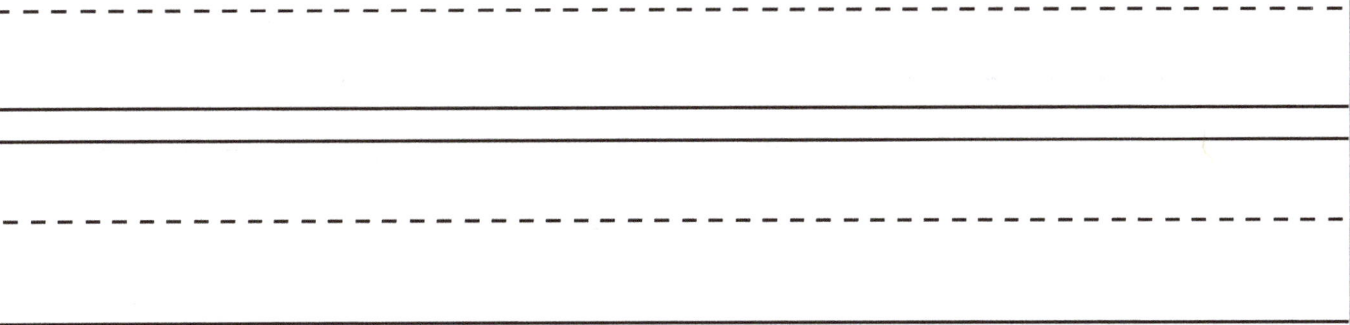

Trace each letter. Practice writing each letter on your own.

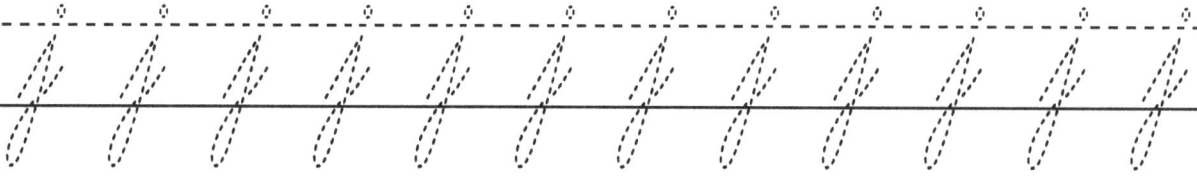

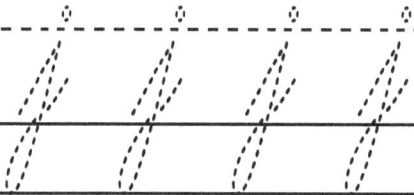

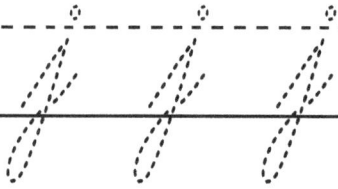

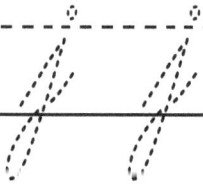

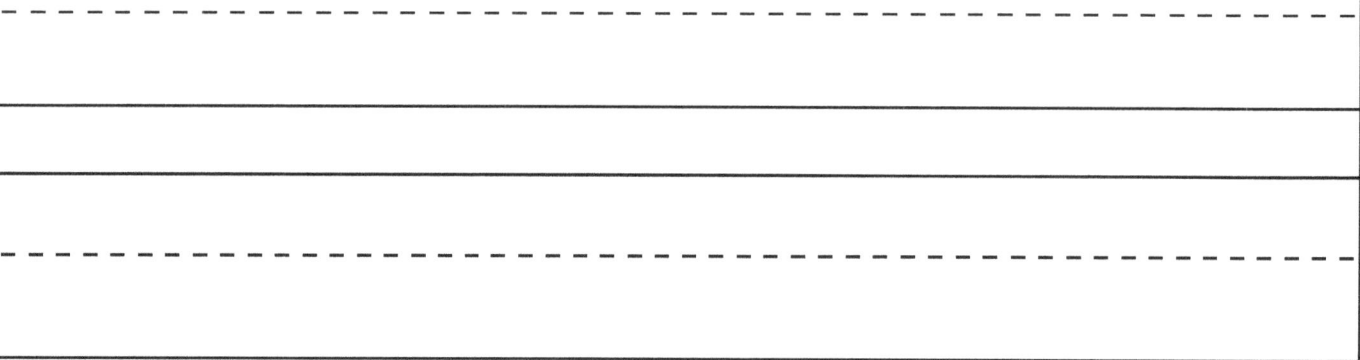

Trace each letter. Practice writing each letter on your own.

$\mathcal{K}$ $\mathcal{K}$ $\mathcal{K}$ $\mathcal{K}$ $\mathcal{K}$ $\mathcal{K}$ $\mathcal{K}$ $\mathcal{K}$ $\mathcal{K}$ $\mathcal{K}$ $\mathcal{K}$

$\mathcal{K}$ $\mathcal{K}$ $\mathcal{K}$ $\mathcal{K}$

$\mathcal{K}$ $\mathcal{K}$ $\mathcal{K}$

$\mathcal{K}$ $\mathcal{K}$

$\mathcal{K}$

Trace each letter. Practice writing each letter on your own.

k *k* *k* *k* *k* *k* *k* *k* *k* *k*

k *k* *k* *k*

k *k* *k*

k *k*

k

Name:_____ Date:_____

Trace each letter. Practice writing each letter on your own.

Trace each letter. Practice writing each letter on your own.

b b b b b b b b b b b b b

b b b b

b b b

b b

b

Trace each letter. Practice writing each letter on your own.

m m m m m m m m

m m m m

m m m

m m

m

Name:_____ Date:_____

Trace each letter. Practice writing each letter on your own.

m *m* *m* *m* *m* *m* *m* *m* *m* *m*

m *m* *m* *m*

m *m* *m*

m *m*

m

Name:_____ Date:_____

Trace each letter. Practice writing each letter on your own.

n n n n n n n n n n

n n n n

n n n

n n

n

Trace each letter. Practice writing each letter on your own.

m m m m m m m m m m

m m m m

m m m

m m

m

Trace each letter. Practice writing each letter on your own.

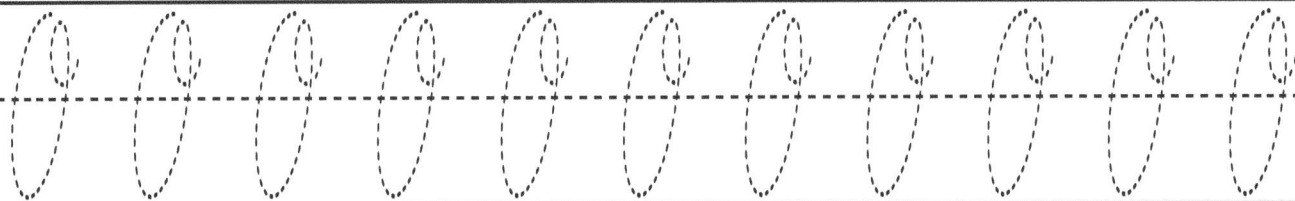

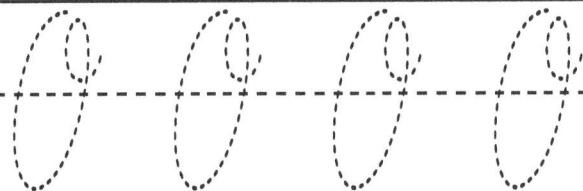

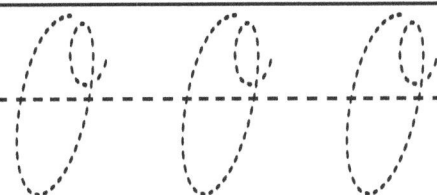

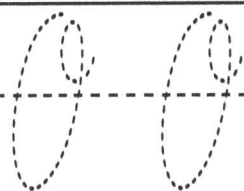

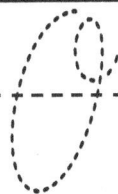

Trace each letter. Practice writing each letter on your own.

b b b b b b b b b b b b

b b b b

b b b

b b

b

Trace each letter. Practice writing each letter on your own.

_p_ _p_ _p_ _p_ _p_ _p_ _p_ _p_ _p_ _p_ _p_ _p_

_p_ _p_ _p_ _p_

_p_ _p_ _p_

_p_ _p_

_p_

Trace each letter. Practice writing each letter on your own.

p p p p p p p p p p p p

p p p p

p p p

p p

p

Trace each letter. Practice writing each letter on your own.

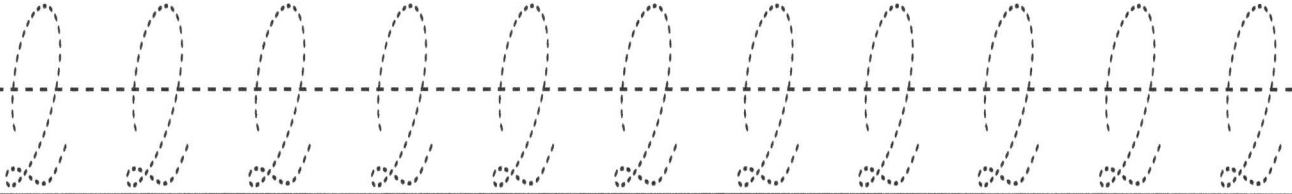

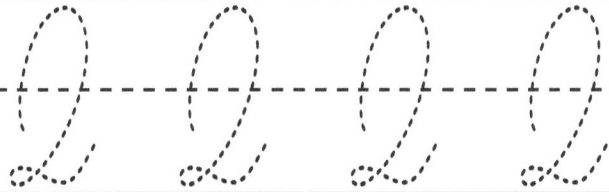

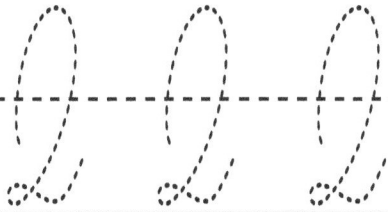

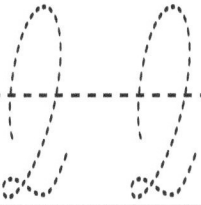

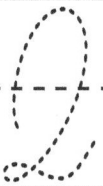

Trace each letter. Practice writing each letter on your own.

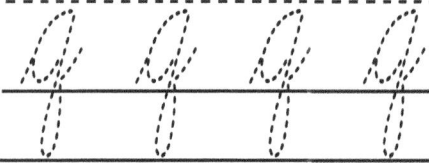

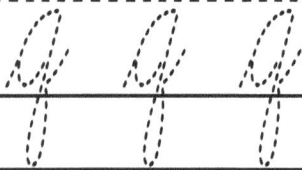

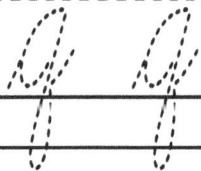

Trace each letter. Practice writing each letter on your own.

$\mathcal{R}$ $\mathcal{R}$ $\mathcal{R}$ $\mathcal{R}$ $\mathcal{R}$ $\mathcal{R}$ $\mathcal{R}$ $\mathcal{R}$ $\mathcal{R}$ $\mathcal{R}$ $\mathcal{R}$ $\mathcal{R}$

$\mathcal{R}$ $\mathcal{R}$ $\mathcal{R}$ $\mathcal{R}$

$\mathcal{R}$ $\mathcal{R}$ $\mathcal{R}$

$\mathcal{R}$ $\mathcal{R}$

$\mathcal{R}$

Trace each letter. Practice writing each letter on your own.

Name:_____ Date:_____

Trace each letter. Practice writing each letter on your own.

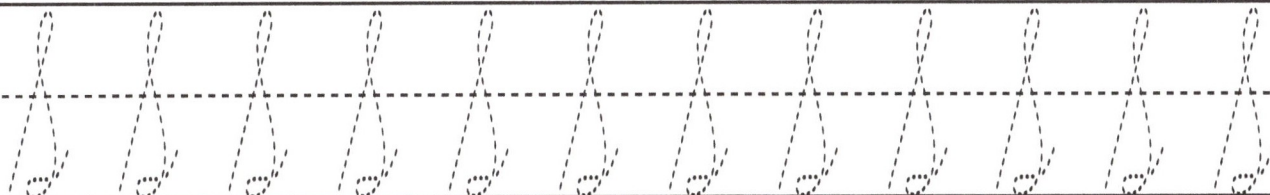

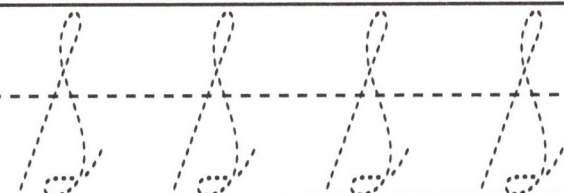

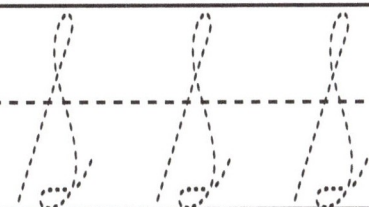

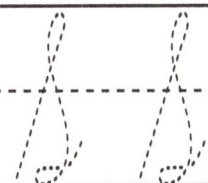

Name:_____ Date:_____

Trace each letter. Practice writing each letter on your own.

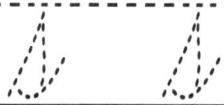

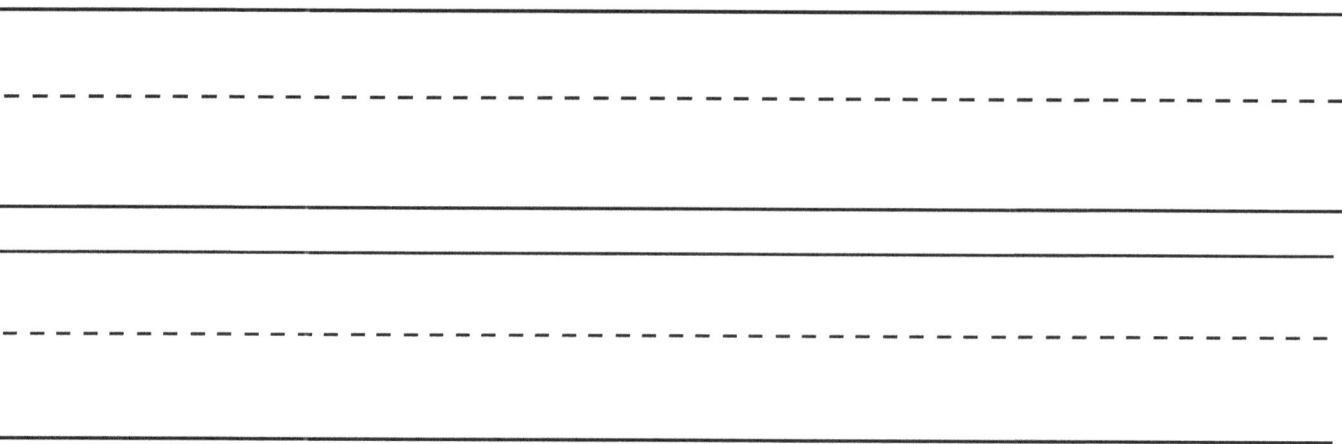

b b b b b b b b b b b b b

b b b b

b b b

b b

b

Name:_____ Date:_____

Trace each letter. Practice writing each letter on your own.

$\mathscr{T}$ $\mathscr{T}$ $\mathscr{T}$ $\mathscr{T}$ $\mathscr{T}$ $\mathscr{T}$ $\mathscr{T}$ $\mathscr{T}$ $\mathscr{T}$ $\mathscr{T}$

$\mathscr{T}$ $\mathscr{T}$ $\mathscr{T}$ $\mathscr{T}$

$\mathscr{T}$ $\mathscr{T}$ $\mathscr{T}$

$\mathscr{T}$ $\mathscr{T}$

$\mathscr{T}$

Trace each letter. Practice writing each letter on your own.

t t t t t t t t t t t

t t t t

t t t

t t

t

Trace each letter. Practice writing each letter on your own.

$\mathcal{U}$ $\mathcal{U}$ $\mathcal{U}$ $\mathcal{U}$ $\mathcal{U}$ $\mathcal{U}$ $\mathcal{U}$ $\mathcal{U}$

$\mathcal{U}$ $\mathcal{U}$ $\mathcal{U}$ $\mathcal{U}$

$\mathcal{U}$ $\mathcal{U}$ $\mathcal{U}$

$\mathcal{U}$ $\mathcal{U}$

$\mathcal{U}$

Trace each letter. Practice writing each letter on your own.

Trace each letter. Practice writing each letter on your own.

Name:_____ Date:_____

Trace each letter. Practice writing each letter on your own.

Trace each letter. Practice writing each letter on your own.

Trace each letter. Practice writing each letter on your own.

Name:_____ Date:_____

Trace each letter. Practice writing each letter on your own.

$\mathcal{X}$ $\mathcal{X}$ $\mathcal{X}$ $\mathcal{X}$ $\mathcal{X}$ $\mathcal{X}$ $\mathcal{X}$ $\mathcal{X}$

$\mathcal{X}$ $\mathcal{X}$ $\mathcal{X}$ $\mathcal{X}$

$\mathcal{X}$ $\mathcal{X}$ $\mathcal{X}$

$\mathcal{X}$ $\mathcal{X}$

$\mathcal{X}$

Trace each letter. Practice writing each letter on your own.

N N N N N N N N N N N N N

N N N N

N N N

N N

N

Name:_____ Date:_____

Trace each letter. Practice writing each letter on your own.

Trace each letter. Practice writing each letter on your own.

Trace each letter. Practice writing each letter on your own.

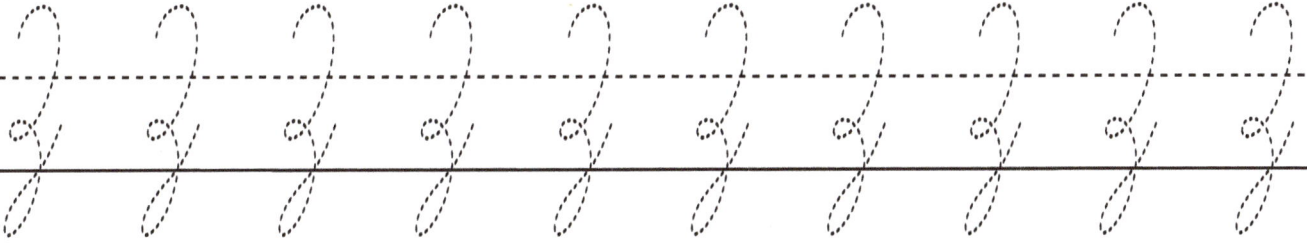

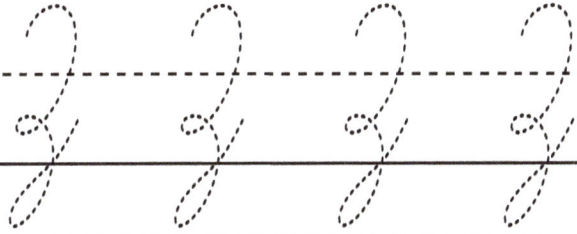

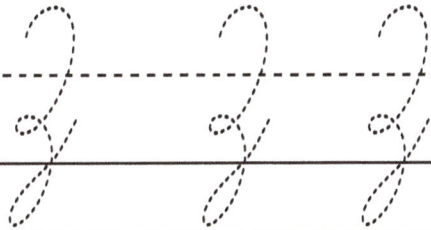

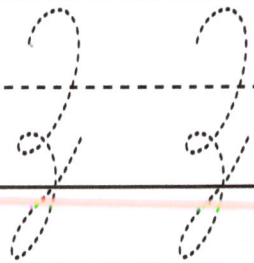

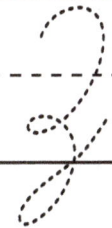

Name:_____ Date:_____

Trace each letter. Practice writing each letter on your own.

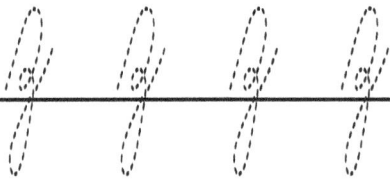

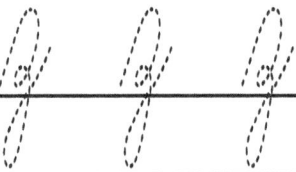

MOVITATIONAL VOCABULARY

1. Courageous – Being very brave by showing courage.

2. Jewel – One that is highly steemed or precious.

3. Noble – Having or showing personal good character traits that other people admire.

4. Original – Being like yourself and not like others; unique.

5. Quintessential – A person who is a perfect example of something.

6. Unique – Being one of a kind; no other person is like you.

7. Victorious – Having won victory and feeling a sense of fuifillment.

8. Witty – Someone or something that is funny and clever.

9. X-factor – A quality or unknown factor that makes someone or something more interesting or valuable.

10. Zestful – A person that has as an energertic and enthusiastic spirit.

DAILY POSITIVE AFFIRMATIONS

I AM AMAZING!
I AM BOLD!
I AM COURAGEOUS!
I AM DETERMINED!
I AM EXCELLENT!
I AM FANTASTIC!
I AM GIFTED!
I AM HONEST!
I AM INTELLIGENT!
I AM A JEWEL!
I AM KIND!
I AM LOVABLE!
I AM MAGNIFICENT!
I AM NOBLE!
I AM ORIGINAL!
I AM POWERFUL!
I AM QUINTESSENTIAL!
I AM RESPECTFUL!
I AM SPECIAL!
I AM TALENTED!
I AM UNIQUE!
I AM VICTORIOUS!
I AM WITTY !
I AM A X-FACTOR!
I AM YOUTHFUL !
I AM ZESTFUL !